Confessions of a Virgin Bride

Kolanda Douglas

For women currently dating, engaged, married or considering marriage, dreaming about marriage, or desiring to be married to a Godly man and praying for Godly success...

For women who did not "get it right" the first time and desire another chance...

Whether you think you are ready for marriage or not, this book is dedicated to you. You can never be too prepared...

Table of Contents

	Page
Foreword	7
Introduction	11
Confession 8: Communication	21
Confession 7: Church	37
Confession 6: In-Laws	51
Confession 5: Career	65
Confession 4: Family	79
Confession 3: Money	97
Confession 2: Sex	107
Confession 1: God	127
Ready. Set. Go!	137
Acknowledgements	145

Foreword

It is a beautiful day! The music is in place. The groomsmen are looking sharp in their tuxedoes and the bridesmaids are blooming like the flowers in their hands. I turn to a nervous groom on my left who seems to be in a state of shock while the doors swing open and his angelic bride comes gliding down the aisle on the arm of her father. Then I say it, my words setting the tone, "Dearly beloved, we are gathered here today..." The audience is smiling, some are even crying. It is my initial chance to bring gravity to the ceremony. Therefore, I recite the following words from my black book: "Marriage is an honorable estate, instituted of God, blessed by our Lord Jesus Christ, and declared by Saint Paul to be honorable among men. It is not, therefore, to be entered into without Holy advice, or lightly, but reverently, soberly, advisedly, and in the fear of God."

As a Pastor, I have experienced this many times; each time hoping the seriousness of the opening words of the ceremony will sink in and last for a lifetime. I spoke the same words at Kolanda's wedding to her husband, Marcus, and I could not be more proud of them. Like many Pastors and others who perform marriage ceremonies, I realize the importance of pre-marital counseling and the sober contemplation of marriage beforehand.

In *Confessions of a Virgin Bride*, Kolanda has taken the opening wedding statement to another level. She is sounding the alarm, encouraging single women to prepare themselves for marriage and wedded women to maintain their commitment. Reading her words is as if the reader is holding Kolanda's hand as she takes them on a journey of enlightenment and preparation.

On this book's journey, Kolanda takes us to key and pertinent areas of marriage. These are areas that can make or break a union and are sometimes hard to talk about. Yet, she confronts them head-on and gives us important points to remember. She makes us feel comfortable as she lets down all pretenses and shares her faults as well as her victories. Her experiences become clear illustrations that synchronize with her key points to make an indelible impression.

Kolanda does not forget that successful marriages begin and end with the creator of marriages- God. She plants each area of exploration into scripture, and juxtaposes each word of advice to the Biblical text. This allows the reader to do personal follow-ups in his/her Bible time so God can speak more to his/her heart.

The "his/her" in the last sentence was intentional. That is because this book is widespread in application. Though Kolanda specifically designed it for single women and newly married brides, it is just as useful for single men and new grooms. Even "not-so-newlywed" and mature couples can benefit from the real world truths they can easily identify. This is a great handbook for marriage counselors, group book studies, marriage ministries, and Christian dating seminars (and the list goes on.) Kolanda's perspective as a "virgin bride" and learning wife is far reaching and a must for many.

I have had the privilege of knowing Kolanda and Marcus and watching them grow up. It was evident early that each was special and bound for God's use of them in special ways. It has been no surprise their marital union has yielded a unique ministry inspiring many. I believe that Kolanda is not just writing, but she is fulfilling purpose. The author carries out her God-given assignment to inform us as readers and does so in a way that allows us to realize how problems can be stepping-stones for improvement if we keep trying and listen closely to the Holy Spirit.

Pastor Donald E. Sheppard, Ph.D.

Introduction

"Any person who is uninitiated, uninformed, or the like," this is the definition Webster has for a virgin.

As the title suggests, I was a virgin bride when I married and I was more of a virgin than I realized. When most people hear of a virgin, they automatically think of sex. Well, through years of marriage, I have come to realize I was a virgin in a lot of areas.

Now, with respect to sex and intimacy, trying to abstain, that does not mean I was innocent; I was not. There was plenty of handholding, hugging and heavy kissing prior to marriage. Though I am proud to have the testimony of being a virgin bride, it was not an easy achievement. There were many times I wanted to give in, relieve my frustration, and give my body what it craved. "Lord, keep me even when I don't want to be kept," was my prayer. Thankfully, that prayer covered me during the tough times and kept me until my long-awaited wedding night.

I married my high school sweetheart, Marcus, aka Superman, at the age of 22. If you have read my other book, *Church Girls Just Want to Have Fun*, then you have an idea of how we came to be. Marcus proposed in 2008 on Christmas Day; I was a junior in college. Growing up, I never imagined I would get engaged while still attending college. However, it was the next step in our relationship given the number of years we had been dating.

When choosing the wedding date for 2010, we decided to select a number of significance. You see, by the time we would be married, Marcus and I would have been dating for seven years. Seven is the number of completion; the number after seven is eight. I researched the significance of the number eight and learned it is the number of new beginnings. Perfect! We agreed after completing seven years of dating, the new beginnings of marriage should follow thereafter. However, the only Saturday in 2010 that fell on the eight day of the month was in May- a week after my college graduation. What a coincidence!

During the time most women are preparing for marriage, I was completing my senior year of college. I was a full-time student working to finish my internship and working part-time as a Substitute Teacher and Resident Assistant. Honestly, I did not have the mental, emotional or financial capacity to prepare for marriage. I also neglected to make time for the Holy Spirit to teach me about my impending transition from singleness to marriage. Any reserve energy and time I could muster was given to my wedding planner.

Some people believe marriage is a journey that should be explored and travelled by the husband and wife- alone. Actually, I was one of those people. During the year and a half Marcus and I were engaged, not one married couple *willingly* took us under their care to offer support, advice or teaching. In fact, my first serious discussion about marital concerns was in premarital counseling, three months prior to our wedding. Consequently, I concluded that marriage was a step Marcus and I would have to discover and conquer together- but alone.

How scary!

The first year of our marriage was a tailspin. After the "new car smell" wore off after about six months, I had no idea who I had married. He was completely different from the person I had dated for seven years. With all the arguing, fighting for control and refusal to submit, I spent the latter part of our first year asking God if I had made a mistake. "Lord, if things are this hard maybe I misunderstood Your direction. Was my relationship with Marcus for dating only? Was I supposed to marry someone else?" I remember asking my mother on numerous occasions, "Why did you and daddy let me do this?" Embarrassed our first year of marriage was not turning out the way I had imagined, I did not reach out to anyone. I was ashamed. After all, the first year is supposed to be the honeymoon stage, right?

By the second and third years of marriage, the trivial to medium-sized kinks in our relationship had either been accepted or compromised. I no longer cared about the empty water bottles or dirty socks he would leave all over the house and he had accepted my used tissues under my pillow when I was not feeling well and that I had an opinion on every decision he made. However, the larger strains on our marriage remained unaddressed. With no new perspectives to consider, no one to consult, and my shame increasing, we were at an impasse.

It was a month before our fourth wedding anniversary that I realized we would not make it another year, alone. Still, I refused to reach out to someone for help. It was our marriage, our problems, our business. Yet, one day after a massive argument, Marcus reached out to his friend, John, for advice. John called his wife, Jessica, and asked her to contact me.

That phone call from Jessica changed my life and transformed my marriage. We exchanged greetings then she asked me to meet her at a local bookstore. Humiliated that she already knew the details of our argument, I did not trust myself to not become emotional in public while speaking with her. Hence, I asked to sit in her car instead of going inside.

"Hey, how's everything going?" I asked, attempting small talk. "We have to double date soon. We haven't hung out in a while."

"John told me what happened," Jessica said, getting to the point.

"So, he told you what Marcus did?" I interrupted as immediate embarrassment filled up the space. "Can you believe him?"

"He told me everything," Jessica continued. "I know your heart is broken but your marriage does not have to end because of this."

Instantly, the dams of my heart and the walls of my shame broke. I was tired of fighting to conceal my embarrassment and uphold my pride. I cried like a baby as she encouraged and prayed for me. Before we departed, she gave me a marriage workbook full of scriptures and activities to help me understand and appreciate my role as a wife. We met weekly until I completed the workbook and she coached me on the topics most difficult to grasp. That day sealed our friendship and her position as my accountability partner.

What's Inside?

Titus 2:4-5 commissions, *"...that they admonish the young women to love their husbands, to love their children, to be discreet, chaste, homemakers, good, obedient to their own husbands, that the word of God may not be blasphemed."*

As Jessica responded to this commission for my sake, I intend to do the same with *Confessions of a Virgin Bride*. If more wives would teach, encourage, and confess their mistakes to one another as these verses instruct, I am convinced it may adequately prepare single women for marriage and help married women uphold their commitment. Additionally, it may eliminate common arguments and heartache within Christ-centered marriages.

My experiences regarding the major, yet intangible, life altering, mind-blowing, heart-changing transition from singleness to marriage birthed this unofficial, informal marriage diary of mine. Inside you will discover eight confessions about marriage I wish I would have learned or addressed before entering into the lifetime covenant. I wish someone would have explained and preached these confessions to me before I married. In the pages to come, I will focus on the following areas and confess my faults within each so you will learn from my experiences: Communication, Church, In-Laws, Career, Family, Money, Sex and God.

Each confession ends with a section titled, *Confess Your Faults*, which provides scriptures, a self-exam, a short prayer and confession to initiate your personal time with the Lord. The scriptures provided indicate the Biblical standard for the confession. In some instances, the scripture offers Biblical encouragement for the confession because change and progression can be challenging. Every marital concern we may encounter is directly or indirectly referenced in the Bible. God's Word provides wisdom for every issue because *"...we do not have a High Priest who cannot sympathize with our weaknesses, but was in all points tempted as we are, yet without sin." (Hebrews 4:15 NKJV)*

The bible admonishes us to, ***"Confess your trespasses to one another, and pray for one another, that you may be healed. The effective, fervent prayer of a righteous man avails much." (James 5:16 NKJV)*** It is for this reason, in the Confess Your Faults sections, while you will not confess to a group, you will confess to yourself and know that I will be praying for you and your healing as you move towards self-reflection. Preparing spiritually, emotionally and mentally for marriage is an individual quest.

The self-exams are designed to identify areas in which you may need to change, improve or address. One of the most important, mind-blowing, but simple, lessons marriage has taught me is, I cannot change Marcus. No matter how much I complain, cry or beg, I do not possess that level of power. I can only change me. Whenever the Holy Spirit reveals bad habits, behaviors, beliefs, etc., He gives me the power to change, improve or address them. Thankfully, change can be infectious. Your husband may also decide to change due to the changes he witnesses in you.

People often begin relationships without knowing themselves. They may not know their career goals or their stance on specific issues but they know they do not want to be alone. Yet, it is difficult to learn and serve another while you are distracted with learning yourself.

It is my desire that by reading this book and completing the *Confess Your Faults* sections, you will be able to address these confessions prior to marriage or readdress them if you are currently married. After reading the final page, I pray you will:

- Determine whether you are spiritually, mentally and emotionally prepared to partake in the covenant of marriage and fulfill your duty as a wife
- Discern the spiritual condition of your relationship to the extent that you and your husband are familiar with the spiritual account and commitment of one another
- Identify disparities that may disqualify the relationship from marriage
- Access the readiness of the relationship to transition to marriage
- Understand the need for sexual purity prior to marriage and the responsibility of sexual intimacy within marriage

Of course, there are marriage related concerns you will not be able to tackle until you are married. Still, there are concerns in which you need to establish your personal standard now. The best time to prepare for marriage is when you are single. During your singleness, you are without distraction from a partner and the possibility to be persuaded by their way of thinking. It is a time to discover what you need and desire in a spouse. It is a time to discover areas that are nonnegotiable and areas you are willing to negotiate. Set your standards, determine your boundaries, and establish your plan now.

I wish I could tell you there is a secret formula to obtaining a Godly-successful marriage. I wish I could tell you there is a one-for-all model husbands and wives can follow to guarantee marital bliss. However, those things do not exist. The truth is, you have to use Godly wisdom and apply it accordingly in your marriage. *"If any of you lacks wisdom, let him ask of God, who gives to all liberally and without reproach, and it will be given to him." (James 1:5 NKJV) "Wisdom is the principal thing; therefore get wisdom. And in all your getting, get understanding." (Proverbs 4:7 NKJV) "...wisdom is better than rubies, and all the things one may desire cannot be compared with her." (Proverbs 8:11 NKJV)*

As I pour out my heart in each confession, I pray it breeds clarity, knowledge, encouragement, practical application, wisdom and discernment. I am grateful my husband has given me his blessing to share some of our struggles and I am hopeful *Confessions of a Virgin Bride* will be the resource and lifeline in which you have been searching.

Confession 8: Communication

"After countless destructive arguments riddled with disrespectful banter, I confess that mutually beneficial, respectful, effective communication is key for a Godly-successful marriage."

Before I got married, I believed I was a great speaker. I had won countless awards for public speaking over the years confirming my abilities. Achieving award-winning status as a speaker has to account for something, right?

Unfortunately, I did not understand that possession of public speaking skills did not guarantee I would be a perfect communicator in my marriage. There were many occasions I used my skills to outtalk and over talk Marcus.

Growing up, I was a self-proclaimed "Daddy's Girl" and wore the title proudly. My father never said *"No"* to my sister and me. He worked hard, long hours so he compensated for his time away from us by never saying "No" to our requests. Since this was my upbringing for 21 years before I married at 22, it influenced the perception of my husband.

One day, I told Marcus I wanted to buy new clothes to revive my wardrobe. His response? "No."

"What do you mean?" I asked with my voice raised. "No as in not today but maybe tomorrow or next week, right?"

"No, as in no you can't buy new clothes," Marcus replied with an elevated voice.

"Well, I need a better reason than that. My daddy never said *"No"* so if you're going to say it then tell me why the answer is no," I replied angrily.

"I don't have to explain that to you," he replied before walking away.

"I'm not your child, you can't just tell me "*No*" without an explanation!" I yelled.

Looking back, I must confess, despite my public speaking success, I was not a very good communicator. I simply did not understand the process of communication and I underestimated its power. *James 3:6* warns, *"And the tongue is a fire, a world of iniquity. The tongue is so set among our members that it defiles the whole body, and sets on fire the course of nature; and it is set on fire by hell."* If utilized negatively, communication can produce adverse effects. According to *James 3:10*, *"Out of the same mouth proceed blessing and cursing. My brethren, these things ought not to be so."* Therefore, communication is a learned behavior.

Are you aware there is an art to communication and it should be practiced skillfully to produce desirable results? Oftentimes, people have a tendency to overlook that part of the process.

Although communication is a natural behavior, training is needed. For example, a baby naturally babbles and coos; it is their form of speaking. However, if that baby is to ever be understood, it must continue practicing until their babbles and coos are transformed into a known language.

What is communication?

Did you know communication is one of the leading causes for divorce? Essentially, marriages can survive health issues, infidelity, infertility, death of children or even bankruptcy; however, marriages cannot survive a lack of communication. This process is so vital to the lifeline of the relationship it is required in every fragment. The entire relationship must be knitted together by the practice of effective communication. In fact, every confession in this book is hinged upon this theory. Hence, we are beginning with the confession of communication because the remaining confessions are useless if this one is not achieved.

It is important to note that communication alone is not sufficient. Anyone who has learned to talk, write, use sign language or even text is able to communicate. Yet, possession of the skill does not mean it is utilized skillfully. The *skill* of communication must be coupled with a learned practice of *effective* communication.

Scientifically speaking, communication is the process of conveying a message in a clear manner. This is the result of effective communication. While the scientific depiction of the process seems simple, communication is one of the hardest processes to follow and achieve as a human being.

Communication is not a linear process. A linear process implies either a fixed end or an ongoing message from the sender only. See below:

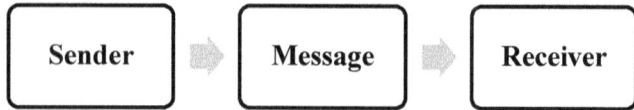

Sender	→	Message	→	Receiver

As shown, this process grants permission to the sender to end the process after their message is delivered. Dictators typically gravitate toward this model. Additionally, it does not provide an opportunity for the receiver to respond. Here is an example:

"I had a dream last night about our future," Marcus mentioned. "I think it's time for us to move to another location; I'm going to start looking as soon as possible."

Opening my mouth to speak, I simply watched Marcus walk away without saying anything.

This scenario demonstrates the communication of a linear process. Marcus, the sender, sent a message to me, the receiver, about moving. As the model suggests, Marcus determined the end of the communication process by walking away. Consequently, I must decode a message that affects me, without any validation from Marcus to indicate I interpreted it correctly. I received the message without an opportunity to provide feedback or ask questions. Thus, this model is likely to produce misinterpretation, miscommunication and resentment. Obviously, linear communication is not mutually beneficial, respectful or effective in marriage.

Conversely, the process of effective communication is circular, connected, repetitive and continuous. It is a mutually beneficial process that grants the sender and the receiver the opportunity to express and provide feedback. This model indicates value in whatever the sender and receiver contribute, regardless of who initiated the process. It encourages both parties to share comfortably with one another and confront challenging topics rather than avoiding conflict.

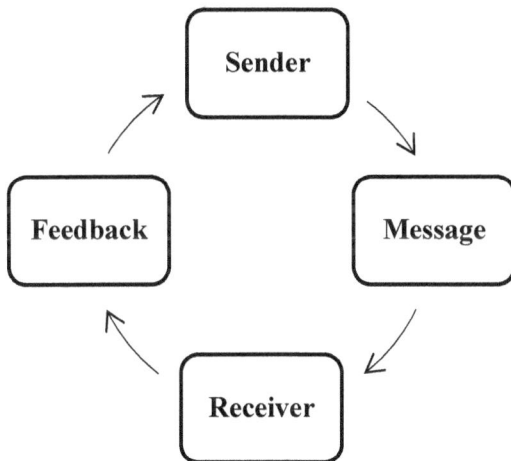

The process of effective communication begins when the Sender, using their experiences, attitudes and perceptions, encodes or converts a message to the Receiver using a medium such as face-to-face, telephone, texting, email, etc. Next, the Receiver, using their experiences, attitudes and perceptions, decodes or interprets the message. Then, the Receiver encodes a message for feedback to the Sender. Finally, the Sender interprets the feedback to restart the process again until the initial message is communicated clearly. Here is an example:

"I had a dream last night about our future," Marcus mentioned. "I think it's a great time for us to move, I'm going to start looking now."

Opening my mouth to speak, I swallowed hard. "Wait a minute, what do you mean it's time to move? What kind of dream was it?"

"The Lord showed me it's time to start expanding our family." Marcus explained. "I believe it was a sign. If we do, we'll need a bigger place."

"Well, thank God for the sign and the confirmation, we've been praying for." I said, squeezing Marcus' hand. "This will give us an opportunity to get prepared and established before we welcome a new baby to our family."

"I agree," Marcus replied.

"I'll start researching moving companies," I said.

"Thanks for trusting me," Marcus said before walking away.

This scenario demonstrates effective communication. Again, Marcus sent the message to me about moving. Yet, with this process, I had an opportunity to ensure I interpreted the message correctly by asking questions and providing feedback. As a result, both my husband and I end the communication process respectfully and with a mutual understanding about the matter and how to move forward. Interestingly, as you can see, I even offered Marcus my physical support in addition to emotional support.

What type of communicator are you?

Do you know? Although the process of effective communication does not change, our personality and presentation of the process can influence the desired result. Consequently, it is important to know how you communicate the process. Recognizing how you communicate then understanding how your husband communicates can prevent miscommunication. There are four types of communicators:

1. **Observer:** Calms tense situations; prefers not to confront issues unless really upset; passive

2. **Achiever:** Wants to be the winner; does not consider the feelings and/or the opinions of others; competitive; aggressive

3. **Explosive:** Cold exterior with a fiery interior; does not confront issues openly when they do not agree; passive aggressive

4. **Connector:** Expresses needs clearly; listens to others before determining a conclusion; nurturing and sensitive; assertive

If you are an observer communicator and your husband is an achiever, the likelihood that your communication would be effective and mutually beneficial is slim. You may often feel ignored and depreciated due to your lack of expressing your feelings and your husband's over-expression of his feelings and his need to win the debate. Similarly, the communication process is in danger for the explosive wife married to a connector. Although the husband would be able to express himself sensibly, the wife may often feel annoyed about issues due to her lack of expression about her feelings and would most likely hold it against her husband.

Whether you identify with these scenarios or not, I am not saying the marriage will not be successful or even that the relationship should be severed. However, if each party does not make positive adjustments to their style, it can be detrimental to the health of the relationship. It is similar to a person who lives with an illness. Though the person continues to live, the illness affects their overall health status. Living does not invalidate the fact that the person is still sick. Likewise, what is a marriage if the husband and wife do not communicate effectively? How will they agree on pursuits that affect them mutually? How will they agree to purchase a home, a car, start a family, raise children, etc. without the ability to communicate well?

What's the point?

Although the model of effective communication is perfect, there is no perfect communicator. Despite our best efforts to communicate clearly, the way we encode or decode the message is involuntarily filtered through our experiences, attitudes and perceptions. Your mood, energy level, surroundings, etc. can affect the tone in which the message is communicated. Consequently, the receiver tends to provide feedback based on the message and the delivery combined rather than the message alone. Think about it, if you have had a terrible day at work then your response to your husband's everyday question, "Honey, what's for dinner?" may be expressed more harshly than usual.

Upon reflection, there is a perfectly good explanation to why I did not receive a "Yes" from Marcus to go shopping: I did not know how to communicate. Specifically, I did not know how to communicate with him. It was not until later in our marriage I realized that depending on the subject, my communication style toggled between achiever and connector. On the contrary, Marcus is an observer. That difference can be extremely frustrating because he often decides not to discuss hot topics right away. Still, that space gives me the chance to think more clearly and be more thoughtful with my response.

Although my experience as a "Daddy's Girl" influenced how I expressed the message, it was likely interpreted as disrespect. If I had been a fully immersed connector communicator and recognized I was married to an observer, I would have translated the message much differently. My approach would have been less direct and not as strong. Although my message was reasonable, the manner in which it was presented was too domineering for a non-confrontational communicator to receive the message. As a result, the ultimate response was provided according to my message and delivery rather than the message alone.

Communication in marriage must be goal-oriented to generate positive effects. There are three goals we should concentrate on when communicating with our husbands:

1. **Spiritual growth**: Use your words to help your husband look more like Christ. ***"Therefore comfort each other and edify one another, just as you also are doing." (I Thessalonians 5:11 NKJV)***

2. **Unity:** Use your words to reach oneness of understanding. *"I, therefore, the prisoner of the LORD, beseech you to walk worthy of the calling with which you were called, with all lowliness and gentleness, with longsuffering, bearing with one another in love, endeavoring to keep the unity of the Spirit in the bond of peace." (Ephesians 4:1-3 NKJV)*

3. **Accountable, compassionate, careful speech:** Use your words to affirm your husband. *"Pleasant words are like a honeycomb, Sweetness to the soul and health to the bones." (Proverbs 16:24 NKJV)*

As women, we have a Biblical responsibility to perfect our communication skills and application of the process. Our communication weighs greatly in the hearts of our families. *"The wise woman builds her house, But the foolish pulls it down with her hands." (Proverbs 14:1 NKJV)* Women set the fragrance of their homes. *"A soft answer turns away wrath, But a harsh word stirs up anger. The tongue of the wise uses knowledge rightly, But the mouth of fools pours forth foolishness." (Proverbs 15:1-2 NKJV)* Your communication, including your personality, actions and attitude, has the ability to build a home full of love, peace, comfort and hope. The type of home your husband will be happy to return to at the end of each day. Or, you can pull it down and your

husband will dread the very existence of your home. You decide.

« CONFESS YOUR FAULTS »

Verses to live by:

✓ *"Let the words of my mouth and the meditation of my heart be acceptable in Your sight, O LORD, my strength and my Redeemer."* Psalms 19:14 NKJV

✓ *"Be gracious in your speech. The goal is to bring out the best in others in a conversation, not put them down, not cut them out."* Colossians 4:6 MSG

✓ *"When I was a child, I spoke and thought and reasoned as a child. But when I grew up, I put away childish things."* I Corinthians 13:11 NLT

Yes/No

1. Do you confront issues in a respectful manner?

2. Do you show respect for the feelings and/or opinions of others even when you disagree?

3. Do you encourage others to talk and ask appropriate questions?

4. Do you make sure you understand what others are trying to communicate?

5. Do you express your ideas clearly so others can understand?

Prayer: Holy Spirit, reveal the areas of my communication style I need to change or improve. Help me to exhibit self-control even when I disagree. I want to be a wife who speaks love, peace and strength to her husband. Amen.

Confession: "Effective communication is the cornerstone of marriage."

Confession 7: Church

"After an arduous season of separate church memberships, I confess that membership at one church, under one doctrine, under one leader, is ideal for a Godly-successful marriage."

Marcus and I grew up in the same Pentecostal church. He was the organist for the youth choir and later became the organist for the church. As he got older, working as an organist became his occupation. When we got engaged, he was working at a Pentecostal church as a pianist; I was a member at another Pentecostal church. Throughout our engagement, we never discussed what would happen with our individual church memberships when we got married.

After the wedding, once we were settled into our home, Marcus made it clear he wanted me to begin attending his church.

"I want my wife at church with me," Marcus explained. "We should be at the same church, worshipping together."

"I don't like that church," I confessed. "I don't learn anything whenever I visit."

"I understand that but we should be at the same church."

"Why don't you join my church?" I suggested.

"I can't quit my job," he said. "We just got married."

Naturally, I felt the same as Marcus and I wanted to comply. I never imagined my husband and I would be split between two congregations. However, I was not fond of his church. Marcus had been attending a traditional Pentecostal church. We grew up in a church similar to it and I did not want to go back. I enjoyed the free worship atmosphere my non-traditional Pentecostal church offered. Therefore, we were at a standstill. We attended separate churches for the first year of marriage because we were at a standstill.

Since Marcus was the pianist at his church, he could never miss a service to attend my church. Although I was not as involved at my church, I did not want to sacrifice my services to attend his church. Unfortunately, the only compromise we could reach was that I would visit his church on fifth Sundays. In hindsight, it was not much of a compromise because fifth Sundays occurred infrequently. Nevertheless, I attended faithfully.

Marcus was happy to know I was in the congregation but I could not help feeling like an outsider. After church ended, I watched him laugh and joke with the other musicians and choir members as I waited for him to pack his equipment. As he left the stage and made his way to me each time, deacons, elders, missionaries, ushers, children and other members of the congregation, stopped him. Marcus had an entire, distinct family that did not include me. It did not register that Marcus would develop close relationships with people I only knew on a cordial level. How could he and I truly be one if I was not a part of his church family? It contradicted our "oneness."

Additionally, by deciding to continue our individual memberships we overlooked many factors that concerned our impending future. For example, which Pastor would counsel us when we needed spiritual advice? Which church would we choose to dedicate our child back to the Lord? Which congregation would we ask to be our child's spiritual village? Which ministry would be entrusted to cultivate our family's spiritual nourishment as a whole? Undoubtedly, these questions should have an appointed resolution before the need transpired.

Don't be Afraid to Ask

Church and religion can become touchy subjects when you are trying to get to know someone. In the past, you could ask a person about their religion and freely disagree. Today, any expression of disagreement is regarded as prejudice and supremacy because we are living in a time where laws are created according to preferences rather than the Bible. As a result, many do not know how to approach the subject of religion without appearing offensive. Unfortunately, some have decided not to discuss the subject at all.

Despite the awkwardness, church and religion should be discussed as soon as possible. If not, the moment you discover you are spiritually incompatible could be more difficult. Why wait until you fall in love with him before you learn he is an atheist? Why wait until your birthday arrives before you learn he will not be celebrating with you because he does not celebrate special occasions and holidays with pagan origins?

Imagine a person applying for a job online. Some companies require applicants to answer prescreening questions before an application can be submitted. The purpose of a prescreening question is to determine whether an application should be extended to an applicant. Depending on the applicant's responses, an opportunity to complete an application may be granted or not. In the same way, you should not extend an application to a man who does not answer your prescreening questions correctly. It is a waste of your time as well as theirs. Here are sample prescreening questions about religion:

- □ Do you believe in God?
- □ What do you believe?
- □ Do you attend church?
- □ What do you believe is important in life?

The initial questions about religion do not have to be in-depth. However, the responses should provide you with enough information to help you make an informed decision about continuing the relationship. Still, if you need additional information, here are a few indirect prescreening questions:

- □ What kind of music do you like?
- □ How do you spend your time on the weekends?

□ How do you celebrate big holidays?

□ What are your family's most cherished traditions?

I had a friend who was getting to know a guy she had met through a mutual friend. He was attractive, educated and employed. Check, check and check. He also had a personal relationship with Christ, regularly attended church, and was involved in the ministry. Check, check and check with bonus points. One day they were talking and he mentioned one of his religious beliefs. He did not believe women should wear jewelry and he did not celebrate pagan holidays such as birthdays or Christmas.

After hearing this, my friend asked other questions to get a better understanding of his beliefs before making a decision about their budding relationship. Eventually, my friend decided she was not willing to adopt his beliefs. It was a nonnegotiable for her. Moreover, adopting his beliefs would also affect their future children. How fortunate was she to discover this information before her heart got involved?

Be willing to ask the deeper questions and also be prepared to move on based on the answers you receive.

Two Hearts, One Flesh

"Do not be unequally yoked together with unbelievers. For what fellowship has righteousness with lawlessness? And what communion has light with darkness?"

II Corinthians 6:14 NKJV

In this passage, the Apostle Paul admonishes believers not to enter into partnership with unbelievers. Why? Imagine a cow and a horse yoked together trying to plow a field. Considering each animal's build, instincts, weight, strengths and weaknesses, it would be impossible for them to plow the field together. Instead of working together, their efforts would be in opposition due to their physical differences.

Like the cow and horse, a believer and unbeliever cannot partner to achieve an objective due to their moral differences. Paul emphasizes this spiritual conflict by noting the impossibility of light uniting with darkness. Even in a movie theater where darkness is standard, the light from the movie illuminates the space. You have never been in a room where one side is completely dark and the other side is completely lit. Why? The two elements cannot exist equally.

This concept of unequally yoked should also be applied to the partnership of marriage. When a believer marries an unbeliever, they are bonding their differences. In essence, it is two people who have decided to journey life together but with two different road maps. Which map is accurate? How will they decide? Clearly, the marriage will be very challenging.

Additionally, being unequally yoked contradicts God's intent for marriage as revealed in ***Genesis 2:24***: ***"Therefore a man shall leave his father and mother and be joined to his wife, and they shall become one flesh."*** To achieve God's intent of becoming "one flesh," the relationship must be so intimate the husband and wife merge into the other literally and figuratively. How can you achieve oneness with someone who opposes what you practice and believe?

The Dangers

Married couples that attend separate churches is not an uncommon circumstance. While I am sure many of them have experienced success, it is not without sacrifice. Marcus and I suffered many things in our respective churches until we finally became members at one church. We have sacrificed date nights for church, mothers introducing him to their single daughters, a woman buying him clothes, a man taking advantage of me for personal gain, and a man wanting to take me on a date.

The decision to continue individual church memberships includes risks. And unfortunately, those risks may not immediately present themselves. When Marcus and I decided not to settle our memberships, we had no idea our relationship would be endangered by a woman buying him clothes as a gift or a man plotting to take me on a date. Underlying risks such as opposing doctrine, competing membership responsibilities, and preying men and women can be hazardous to key components of the marriage and its overall well-being.

Opposing doctrine is risky because what we believe impacts how and what we practice. If the husband and wife are receiving opposing teachings, their differences will eventually intersect. For example, if the husband attends a church that teaches tithe as ten percent of your income that should be given to the church but the wife's church teaches tithe is determined individually and can be given to any entity, tension will surface within their finances. Then, they are likely to condemn one another for disobedience.

Competing membership responsibilities is an additional risk. Churches vary regarding what they expect of lay members, members with titles, and members with positions. For example, as a musician, Marcus was expected to attend weekly routine services and special occasion services. Moreover, he attended weekly choir and band rehearsals. Conversely, as a lay member, I was only expected to attend weekly routine services. Subsequently, I spent countless evenings alone.

Of the three risks, I believe preying men and women is the most important. When a husband or wife regularly attends church without the other, they are susceptible to preying men and women within the congregation. The husband is not present to prohibit lurking men and the wife is not present to prevent devious women. The presence of the husband or wife is needed to ward off men and women with ill intentions. If this risk arises, it has the potential to yield a more widespread effect. It can individually change the husband and wife mentally, physically and emotionally which enflames the entire marriage.

Prior to marriage, I was merely satisfied with the fact that Marcus and I believed in and worshipped the same God. Yet, I should have also considered the church where we would worship our God- together. When deciding the church where you and your husband will commit your spiritual growth, it is important to consider the following:

- □ Does the church in general satisfy you both spiritually? The Pastor? The teaching? The fellowship?
- □ Does the church provide opportunities for each to serve?
- □ Does the church have the capacity to satisfy your children?

☐ Does the church appeal to your non-spiritual interests? Community? Business? Politics? Social justice?

Your church should meet your needs as husband and wife to guarantee mutually-beneficial outcomes. Receiving the same teaching under one leader empowers you as husband and wife. With the combined knowledge and subsequent power of two but as one, you can pray in faith, boldly declare, and rebuke the enemy and expect results. ***Matthew 18:19*** confirms, *"...that if two of you agree on earth concerning anything that they ask, it will be done for them by My Father in heaven."*

« CONFESS YOUR FAULTS »

Verses to live by:

✓ *"And what accord has Christ with Belial? Or what part has a believer with an unbeliever?"* II Corinthians 6:15 NKJV

✓ *"Having a form of godliness, but denying the power thereof: from such turn away."* II Timothy 3:5 KJV

✓ *"To the pure all things are pure, but to those who are defiled and unbelieving nothing is pure; but even their mind and conscience are defiled."* Titus 1:15 NKJV

Yes/No

1. Can you identify the religious beliefs you believe and practice?

2. Can you explain what you believe and why to others?

3. Can you identify the type of church that will satisfy your spiritual needs?

4. Can you identify whether your spirituality is rooted in relationship with Christ or religion?

5. Are your religious beliefs non-negotiable?

Prayer: Holy Spirit, help me to boldly confess what I believe. Despite life's circumstances, help me to hold fast to my faith. If I ever begin to doubt, help me to remember what my spirit already comprehends. Amen.

Confession: "Disharmony means fighting separate wars with less strength. Therefore, spiritual harmony is essential to defeating spiritual warfare as one."

Confession 6: In-Laws

"After reaping the negative effects of not having a relationship with my husband's family, I confess that a personal relationship with your in-laws is crucial for a Godly-successful marriage."

I am always intrigued by women who believe, "I don't care if his mother likes me. As long as he loves me, that's all that matters. I'm marrying him, not her." If this is you, change your thinking immediately! Trust me. If your husband's parents are living and he has a relationship with them, it matters to him whether or not you like them.

You would think after seven years of dating my husband I had a wonderful relationship with his parents before we got married, right? Wrong. The truth is, at the time we began dating, I was only interested in their son and spending time with him. Whatever they knew about me, they learned from Marcus. Our relationship was cordial but formal- nothing more. It was not until Marcus and I married that the status of my relationship with his parents became an issue he wanted to discuss.

"You don't even call my mom," Marcus complained.

"Why do I need to call her?" I asked. "I have a mom."

"That's not the point," he clarified.

"I never called your mom even when we were dating," I explained. "What's changed now?"

"It's just not right. I have a relationship with your mom," he replied. "If you don't have a relationship with my mom, what's going to happen when we start our family?"

"Just because she and I don't have a personal relationship doesn't mean I would keep her from having a relationship with her grandchild."

"We'll see," Marcus said.

"Don't worry about it," I reassured. "Everything will be okay."

We had this discussion a thousand times because I did not understand why he wanted me to have a personal relationship with his parents. In my opinion, I had a relationship with them; it was through Marcus. Whenever he was on the phone with them, I used him to exchange greetings and small talk. Moreover, whenever I saw them, I was always polite and engaging. I even joked with my father-in-law. Yet, it was not enough.

The Family Tree

Developing a relationship with your husband's family can be intimidating. You have to learn how to integrate yourself into his family. At the same time, his family has to learn how to accept you as a new family member. This integration is essential to generating respect and acceptance for your marriage.

I am sure many who believe a relationship with your in-laws is not vital to a marital relationship may use *Genesis 2:24* as their defense. It reads, *"Therefore a man shall leave his father and*

mother and be joined to his wife, and they shall become one flesh. It is important to note the scripture has the phrase, "...leave his father and mother ...," not ignore or forget his father and mother. In context, this verse describes God's design for marriage and His intent for husbands and wives to become one spiritually, mentally and emotionally.

This verse also implies balance is possible. Although difficult, it is possible to leave your family and join your husband while balancing the command to honor your father and mother. Yet, if the parental relationship supersedes the marriage then Biblical unbalance exists and it must be corrected. Your relationship with your parents should not be greater than that with your husband.

Depending on familial circumstances or your husband's personal relationships with his family, a personal relationship with your in-laws may not be possible. Obviously, if his parents are no longer living then a relationship cannot be attained. However, in some instances, an older brother or sister may be regarded as the "parent" so it is important to understand his family's dynamics. Still, if your husband's parents are living and he has a relationship with them, you are likely expected to develop a relationship with them as well.

Relationships with in-laws are often strained due to unexpressed expectations. Here are some questions that may eliminate or diminish the possibility:

☐ Is your family affectionate? Social?

☐ How often would you like to visit our families?

☐ How will we divide our time with our families during holidays?

☐ Do you plan to take family vacations with extended family?

☐ If any, what can we do to minimize disagreements between our families?

☐ Are there any unspoken issues we have with each other's family?

☐ Do you plan to care for aging parents? How?

During one of our premarital counseling sessions, the facilitator described in-laws as two separate trees. Imagine two trees rooted side-by-side in a forest. The differences of height, width, color, fullness, number of branches, etc., between the trees represent the differences between your family and your husband's family. Despite those differences, a branch from one tree must intertwine with a branch from the other tree to create a new tree.

The process of intertwining is an accurate illustration of marriage. One family's upbringing, traditions, preferences are combined with that of another family to produce a new family. In turn, the new family must learn to skillfully combine and compromise their long-standing family differences to live peaceably and successfully as a married couple. This process is so complex and intense you cannot expect it to be achieved overnight. Actually, there is no designated length of time. Nevertheless, it must be accomplished with an intentional, natural progression.

Intertwining my family tree with my husband's family was difficult. Every holiday I spent with my in-laws and away from my family, I took it personally. Every family reunion or banquet I attended, I endured it grudgingly and Marcus noticed. We had countless arguments and I cried many tears but the intertwining process continued despite me.

At the time, the process seemed unreasonably difficult and unbearable. I felt I had to surrender many of my family's traditions and preferences for the sake of submission. Now, I realize the process was difficult due to the lack of a personal relationship with my in-laws. They did not want to take me from my family; they wanted to fully immerse me into their traditions because they were happy to have me as a member of their family. If I had sought the opportunity, a personal relationship with them would have allowed them to demonstrate their intentions sooner. Then, I could have spared Marcus and I those arguments and tears.

Supportive vs. Disruptive Influence

Ideally, like natural parents, in-laws should serve as a supportive influence for the married couple. Their support can be vital to the fragility of a newlywed bond. For couples that have been married longer, their support can help sustain the marriage bond. Additionally, their presence in the couple's life serves as a physical reminder of their marital vows. They would not be designated as in-laws if vows had not been exchanged.

Unlike me, Marcus developed a personal relationship with my mother while we were dating. When we got married, he reached out to her for advice on many occasions. He believed if I did not understand his point of view, perhaps my mother could explain it better. Thankfully, my mother was a supportive influence who remained neutral. She always reminded him, "You told us God told you that Kolanda was your wife. You asked to marry her. Now, go talk to her again and figure it out."

Conversely, in-laws can also be a disruptive influence. They may be disruptive by nature, cause or interference. If they are disruptive by nature, it is typically due to their personality. They may be naturally troublesome, hard to please, uncooperative, etc. Some mothers-in-law simply cannot accept they will no longer be the only woman in their son's life while others will not consider any woman good enough for their son. Therefore, no matter what you do, they are likely to be hard to please and uncooperative because they do not want to the marriage to succeed.

In-laws may be disruptive by cause due to their disagreement about the couple's decisions. For example, a child conceived out of wedlock, living together before marriage or established familial boundaries that upset the overall family dynamic. Additionally, in-laws may be disruptive by cause as a result of a disagreement or argument between husband and wife. While the objective is to have the support of your in-laws, you must be mindful about the marital issues you share with them.

Marcus and I learned this lesson the hard way during the third year of our marriage. One day after a terrible argument, Marcus escaped to the bathroom to put some physical and mental space between us. Well, I did not like that he left me to continue arguing with myself as I yelled at him through the door. I flipped!

I started moving, pushing and dropping things in his studio to give him the illusion I was breaking his equipment. He ran out the bathroom and looked at me with disgust. After a few more angry words, he finally left the house altogether. Then, my father called. He told me Marcus had called both our fathers about my behavior. No doubt Marcus believed I had lost my mind because I was trying to destroy our livelihood.

Days later, after living in silence, I decided to speak up and apologize. Marcus and I reconciled, moved forward and never looked back. However, it took a while before our parents forgot. Sharing your marital issues in times of crisis may seem innocent but then you and your husband will forgive each other and move on. However, your parents may have a difficult time doing the same.

In-laws who are disruptive by interference classically result from unsolicited support and advice. This type of behavior is often viewed as disrespectful or overbearing. For example, the mother-in-law who does not respect boundaries when visiting and reorganizes, redecorates and complains about the cleanliness. Although their intentions may be noble, her behavior could be interpreted as undermining.

It is essential to determine whether your in-laws will be a supportive or disruptive influence in your relationship prior to marriage. The best way to discover their influence is to seek to develop a personal relationship with them before marriage. This can provide you with much needed insight. You may discuss their viewpoints and expectations such as:

- □ What is your perspective about marriage?
- □ What do you believe is the key to a lasting marriage?
- □ What type of wife do you envision for your son?
- □ What type of relationship do you imagine having with your son after he is married?

- What type of relationship do you imagine with your daughter-in-law?
- What type of relationship do you imagine with your grandchildren?

Perhaps you will discover his parents are a disruptive influence and a future relationship is not likely. Or, you may find that relational boundaries need to be discussed and established with them almost immediately. Why wait until marriage to learn your mother-in-law expects to visit whenever she desires?

Finally, developing a personal relationship with your in-laws before marriage eliminates the opportunity for them to make assumptions about you. Naturally, when people do not know anything about you, they make assumptions and create labels to identify you. I know wives who have been accused as domineering, hateful and spoiled by their in-laws. What do they all have in common? They lack personal relationships with their in-laws so they are judged by what is assumed about them.

Regrettably, I did not believe having a personal relationship with my in-laws was vital to the success of my marriage. I did not think it would carry any weight or merit in my marriage. I assumed Marcus would be able to bear his marriage and his parental relationship as two separate, non-connected entities. Thus, I was not overly concerned with addressing or resolving his discontentment.

Eventually, I discovered by not showing an interest to develop a personal relationship with my in-laws, Marcus interpreted it as me not loving him wholly. How could I love him if I was not interested in the persons who nurtured him? How could I appreciate him without appreciating them? Similar to being excluded from his church family, being detached from his natural family also contradicted our oneness. With one simple phone call, my relationship with my in-laws began to blossom and grow. As a result, creating and cultivating a personal relationship with my in-laws only enriched my marriage. Moreover, it seals our unity because there is no opportunity for division from our individual family trees.

« CONFESS YOUR FAULTS »

Verses to live by:

✓ **"Hatred stirs up strife, But love covers all sins."**

Proverbs 10:12 NKJV

✓ **"Love is patient and kind. Love is not jealous or boastful or proud or rude. It does not demand its own way. It is not irritable, and it keeps no record of being wronged. It does not rejoice about injustice but rejoices whenever the truth wins out. Love never gives up, never loses faith, is always hopeful, and endures through every circumstance."**

I Corinthians 13:4-7 NLT

✓ **"Let love be without hypocrisy. Abhor what is evil. Cling to what is good."** *Romans 12:9 NKJV*

Yes/No

1. Are you willing to try to integrate yourself into your husband's family?

2. Do you understand that integration may be successful or unsuccessful?

3. Do you understand that despite the outcome of the integration, it will influence your marriage?

4. Can you respect others even if they do not respect you?

5. Can you love others even if they do not like you?

Prayer: Holy Spirit, help me to genuinely love my husband's family. Reveal any areas in which my love for others needs to be strengthened and help me to change. Even when it is difficult to love, help me to love my neighbors as myself as You command. Amen.

Confession: "In-laws are the roots from which my new family will grow. I will not neglect them which can kill the tree but cultivate the roots, expecting growth."

Confession 5: Career

"After thoughtlessly disrupting our family vision and inserting new ambitions, I confess that a mutual understanding of career goals is beneficial for a Godly-successful marriage."

This confession is an area in which I recently had to repent and ask my husband for forgiveness after nearly five years of marriage. I did not realize and could not verbalize my career path, plan or goals until I had our son in 2015. By the time I reached my senior year in high school, I knew I was good at two things: writing and public speaking. With those strengths in mind, I went to college and majored in Communication. Then, when I could not find any employment, I went to graduate school and majored in a higher level of communication- Mass Media Arts and Journalism. Shortly after, I found gainful employment and was satisfied until I learned I was pregnant.

Suddenly, climbing the corporate ladder was no longer important to me. I wanted an opportunity that would not allow me to miss valuable moments of my son's life. So, I told Marcus I wanted to write books and travel the world speaking to diverse audiences about what I had written. He did not take it well.

"I want to quit my job," I announced.

"What do you mean?" Marcus asked, frowning.

"I'm not happy," I explained. "There's no opportunity for promotion so what's the point? And now that we're expecting, I want my son to see me as more than his mommy who works five days a week, eight to five. I want to do something better, something greater."

"You want to quit your job now that we're having a baby?" He asked incredulously. "Does that make sense to you?"

"You're working to live your dream," I justified. "You've always been able to do what you love, I want to do the same."

"We're supposed to be preparing for our son's arrival, not cutting our salary."

"I'm sure we can figure it out if we start planning now," I encouraged.

"No, you're not quitting your job," he replied with frustration.

The onset of anger and disappointment was instant. I felt rejected. He was stifling my aspirations and dismissing my dreams without further discussion or a willingness to try. It seemed as if he was content with me being his wife and our son's mother- nothing more. I panicked; I feared I would be obligated to continue living the life we had created together. The idea of continuing my mundane career routine was both repulsive and frightening.

Still, imagine how Marcus must have felt. I was aware of his career from the beginning; he made sure I was aware of it. He did not have all the details but I knew Marcus wanted to pursue music as his profession before we were engaged. Thus, I married him with the expectation he would be required to attend weekly church services, choir and band rehearsals, special occasion services, and sporadic gigs.

Suddenly, I was interrupting and restructuring his expectation of me. I wanted to cut our combined salary in half to pursue new career plans and still expect him to meet the needs of our growing family. After climbing the corporate ladder for five years with no complaints or ambition, he believed I was satisfied with my career. No doubt he had confidently agreed it was time to expand our family because we both had gainful employment and health benefits. Hearing I was dissatisfied with my life was a shock to him.

For months, I tried to convince Marcus about my plans before our son arrived. Since talking alone was not successful, I wrote my vision on poster board so he could visualize it with me. I also tried to convince him I could not be an effective wife and mother if I was not happy with myself. Despite this, he was not persuaded.

Fortunately, after our son was born, we developed a plan that allowed me to begin shifting career paths. However, it has come with great sacrifice, compromise, consultations and lengthy discussions. We agreed I would not quit my job until I was able to supplement my income. Although it is a reasonable resolution, it required great sacrifice on my end. In addition to taking care of my family, I had to learn how to juggle a full-time job while pursuing my passion part-time.

Seek God

It is not enough to pursue your abilities, talents or interests as a career. If so, you too will suffer from having a general assumption about your future but unable to specify or verbalize your plans. Furthermore, you will be unable to recognize and enter the open doors created for you. Since I did not know any specifics about my career goals, it was difficult to pursue opportunities after graduation because I was not sure which opportunities would complement my unplanned future.

I thought having a general idea about my career goals was sufficient. I was wrong. In retrospect, I was running a race to a finish line in which I did not have the instructions, clues or map to locate. In other words, I was studying, writing papers and working but going nowhere fast.

In addition, possessing a general idea of my career goals provided a skewed image of me to Marcus. It also provided him with a false illusion about our future together. Can you imagine being engaged to a doctor then when you marry he decides he wants to be a lawyer? How problematic would that be? Suddenly, your husband would expect you to offer sacrifice, commitment and money you did not initially perceive. Though it is not impossible to achieve, the unanticipated stress, damaging ultimatums, selfish decision-making or destructive arguments that may arise can be avoided altogether.

In collaboration with recognizing your gifts, seek the Lord about your career path. *Jeremiah 1:5* says, *"Before I formed you in the womb I knew you; Before you were born I sanctified you; I ordained you a prophet to the nations."* I was late in discovering God's purpose for my life but He knew why He created me before I was formed in my mother's womb. The same is true for you. Before you were even introduced to your parents or this world, the Lord knew you.

"But seek first the kingdom of God and His righteousness, and all these things shall be added to you," as found in *Matthew 6:33*. Do not seek success, wealth or promotion; instead, seek His will for your life and your other desires will be an added bonus. If you are living righteously, you can trust God to satisfy your needs. After God reveals your career path, you and your husband can have a more accurate portrayal of your life together and plan accordingly.

Many women decide to wait until they are married before they seize life-changing career opportunities. I have heard excuses such as, "I don't want to accept a position in another city, what if my husband lives here?" Alternatively, "I don't want to start my business now, what if my husband lives in another city?" Do not put your life on hold for a husband who has yet to reveal himself. With an elevated start, you and he can create more together. It is better to meet your husband while you are walking in your destiny; it will give you a better indication of how he will fit into your life.

Similarly, your husband should have career goals. If he does not know his career path when you meet, he must also seek the Lord for direction. As the provider, it is important for him to have a system by which he will provide prior to marriage. You may ask:

- What are you passionate about?
- What are your career goals?
- How do you plan to achieve those goals?
- What is the time commitment?
- Describe a typical day of working your dream career.
- What is the longevity for that type of career?
- Does your career permit the liberty of raising a family? Travel?
- How do you imagine your wife helping you pursue your career?
- How will our careers impact one another?
- Are you willing to adjust your work schedule in exchange for increased family time?

Perhaps the responses will give you a better indication of how you will fit or if you can fit into his life. In addition, the responses may reveal a lack of passion, drive or ambition. If so, this revelation may hint to a lack of passion in other areas as well. While it is possible he may discover and pursue his career after marriage, the transition can be difficult. Like any unforeseen circumstance, the interruption into your established routine requires adjustment.

People make countless life-changing decisions on impulse. They begin relationships, start businesses, buy houses, purchase cars, and even quit their jobs based on a hunch- not an assurance. As a result, the decision usually ends in regret or consequence. This is what occurs when we make decisions without consulting God. Nevertheless, if you *"Delight yourself also in the LORD, He shall give you the desires of your heart." (Psalms 37:4 NKJV)*

Ambition teaches us to work hard to be successful and fulfilled. Still, there is no way to know the future outcome of your decisions so you must seek the One who does. *"For I know the thoughts that I think toward you, says the LORD. "They are plans for good and not for disaster, to give you a future and a hope." (Jeremiah 29:11 NKJV)* The only way you will attain real success is by yielding to God's purpose for your life. *"There are many plans in a man's heart, Nevertheless the Lord's counsel—that will stand." (Proverbs 19:21 NKJV)* As you exchange your plans for His plans and submit your will to His will, *"May He grant you according to your heart's desire, And fulfill all your purpose." (Psalms 20:4 NKJV)*

Write the Vision

After seeking the Lord regarding my career path and receiving confirmation, Marcus and I created a vision board. We listed both personal and family goals that were specific, measurable and achievable. In addition, we noted the month and year we planned to complete each goal. It was beneficial to see what Marcus desired for himself and our growing family. It was also enlightening to know which months the other would need added support and encouragement. When we finished the board, we posted it in our bedroom to serve as a constant reminder of our purpose.

Once Marcus and I reached an understanding about our combined visions, it was important for me to write the vision. We wanted to exercise *Habakkuk 2:2* literally: *"...Write the vision and make it plain on tablets, That he may run who reads it."* By writing our goals on the vision board plainly, we sealed the vision in our minds and made it clearer to ourselves. Moreover, the physical board cannot be misinterpreted or distorted; the vision is clear.

It is easy to become sidetracked or discouraged when fulfilling your purpose. Along the path, I have experienced distractions such as non-related, enticing job offers and interruptions such as surgery, car accidents and more. Still, the vision board was a visible reminder about the One who created my path and walked it before me. *"[His] word is a lamp to my feet and a light to my path." (Psalms 119:105 NKJV)* Further, the board helped me sift through opportunities to identify and attain those designed for me.

What would have happened if I had been seeking the Lord about my career from the beginning? Who would I be today? Where would I be today? How much further along in my career would I be? How would it have enhanced my marriage? How would it have benefited Marcus to know my career goals from the beginning? How would that have profited him as a provider? At this point, these are questions only God can provide answers. Thankfully, *"...all things work together for good to those who love God, to those who are the called according to His purpose." (Romans 8:28 NKJV)*

Before I married Marcus, I always imagined how I would fit into his career. The image was never clear since I was not aware of my purpose but I always saw myself standing at a podium while he played the organ. I always knew our purposes would collide and allow us to minister together. Similarly, you and your husband's careers should be complementary. The career paths should not be competing or distracting to ignite selfishness or division. Instead, the careers should work together for the benefit of your family.

Though you may pursue your careers individually, it is ultimately one ministry, from one flesh, for the glory of God.

« CONFESS YOUR FAULTS »

Verses to live by:

✓ **"And those who know Your name will put their trust in You; For You, *LORD*, have not forsaken those who seek You."** *Psalms 9:10 NKJV*

✓ **"And you will seek Me and find Me, when you search for Me with all your heart."** *Jeremiah 29:13 NKJV*

✓ **"And whatever things you ask in prayer, believing, you will receive."** *Matthew 21:22 NKJV*

Yes/No

1. Have you sought the Lord about His plans for your life?

2. Do you know your God-ordained purpose?

3. Do you have your career goals written down in a journal, on a vision board, etc.?

4. Have you begun following the career path designed for you?

5. Are you waiting for your husband before you begin pursuing your career?

Prayer: Holy Spirit, reveal the purpose for which I was created. Show me the gifts You have given to me. Help me to walk along the career path you designed specifically for me. I want to be the woman You created me to be; I want to use my gifts for Your kingdom. Amen.

Confession: "I will not allow a dissatisfying career to breed dissatisfaction in other areas of my life."

Confession 4: Family

"After delaying our family momentum due to indecision and oblivion, I confess that a mutual understanding of family planning, gender roles and values are vital for a Godly-successful marriage."

How many times have you been upset with someone because they did not do what you thought they should have done? Perhaps they did not act the way you thought or said something contrary to what you would have said. The resulting disappointment from scenarios such as these typically originates from unspoken expectations.

One of the common but simple areas in marriage that suffers from unstated expectations is family. I am not referring to family as in in-laws but the family established by joining as husband and wife. This area involves family planning, gender roles and values. While this is a major area, it is typically examined at surface level with no thought about its underlying components.

Marcus and I always knew we wanted to expand our family. Then again, we had never established a timeline. We were excited about the possibility of adding a mini-Marcus and mini-Kolanda to our family. We fantasized about how they would look, their personality, and the features we wanted them to gain from us and those we hoped did not continue. We even had baby names selected before we were engaged. And yet, despite that level of dreaming and discussion, we never determined a timeline.

After we were married, we continued to fantasize about our children. However, the conversation changed. Suddenly, there was a need for an established timeline. Marcus wanted to start our family as soon as possible to ensure he would have the health and strength to enjoy his children. On the other hand, I was waiting for a "feeling" to indicate I was ready as well as our marriage, finances and careers. Looking back, my thinking was very flawed. I had no idea what the "feeling" would be or if I would even recognize it. Nevertheless, I was convinced it would come.

After three years of marriage our parents had even begun to inquire about our family planning process. They had even started dropping hints about their readiness to have grandchildren. "Marcus and I need time as husband and wife," I would reply whenever the subject surfaced. "How much time do y'all need?" My mother would ask. "Y'all have been together since you were in ninth grade." "That's not the same," I would answer.

I was right. Knowing Marcus as my boyfriend or even my fiancé was nothing compared to knowing him as my husband. Besides, given the difficulty we had experienced during our initial years of marriage, I was hesitant about making life-changing decisions. I wanted to give us sufficient time for recovery, healing and growth before we expanded our family.

Nevertheless, in June 2014, a month after our fourth wedding anniversary, I decided to stop waiting for the "feeling." I told Marcus I was ready to start our family. I found out I was pregnant that September and our son made his stubborn entrance into the world May 2015- three days after our fifth wedding anniversary. Five is the number of grace. To me, his birth after that anniversary signaled God's free and unmerited favor in our lives despite our marital hardships.

Family Planning

This term means exactly as it reads. Typically, the term is linked to contraceptives and preventing unwanted pregnancies. However, in this instance, family planning refers to actually planning for wanted pregnancies. In addition, other related factors such as timeline and physical, mental and financial preparation.

Although I knew I was not ready for motherhood right away, I did little to prepare for the transition before my son was conceived. I was not mindful of diet and exercise, stress levels or spending habits prior to his birth. Marcus and I lived carefree with sporadic fantasies about our future children. Subsequently, after conception, I was consumed with both personal and physical preparation simultaneously.

After confirming my pregnancy, Marcus and I decided to evaluate our expenses and establish a budget. The conversion to living on a budget was tough because at that point, we had no choice but to make room for new expenses. After gaining weight too fast in the beginning of my pregnancy, I regretted I had not developed an exercise routine prior. After nearly passing out and requiring a prescription for iron later in my pregnancy, I hated I had not been mindful about my diet or acquired healthy eating habits prior.

For effective family planning, you and your husband must first decide whether you will expand your family or not. Some married couples do not desire children at all while others have children from previous relationships and do not desire more. Family planning requires specific, extensive discussions to make well-informed decisions. To begin the process, you may ask:

- Do you want children?
- If we experience trouble conceiving, would you like to adopt or pursue fertility treatments?
- If we do not want children, how will we prevent pregnancy? Contraceptives? Medical procedures?

If you and your husband decide to expand your family, discussions about family planning should not be limited to timeline only. The conversation should also include other factors that will be affected by the growth of the family. In addition, consider future factors that will affect the family.

- How long do you want to wait to have children?
- Are there any health concerns that may impede conception?

- ☐ How many children do you want to have?

- ☐ How will children affect our career goals?

- ☐ How will children affect our financial goals?

- ☐ What core values do you want to instill in our children?

Why wait until you are pregnant to address underlying or familial health issues? Those issues may affect the success or failure of your pregnancy. Why wait until you are pregnant to learn you cannot afford a child and the related expenses? In addition to customary costs such as baby furniture, diapers and formula, there are labor and delivery fees and reoccurring expenses such as doctor visits. Why wait until you are pregnant to learn the bond or emotional health of your marriage is not strong enough to endure an expanding family? Like a runner does not prepare for the race on the day of, do not wait to prepare yourself or your marriage until conception occurs.

Thankfully, experience has taught Marcus and I to now have open discussions. We've decided to set a mutual projected time frame with certain family targets and goals being met before having another baby.

Gender Roles

"To the woman He said: 'I will greatly multiply your sorrow and your conception; In pain you shall bring forth children; Your desire shall be for your husband, And he shall rule over you.'"

Genesis 3:16 NKJV

This penalty was imposed on Eve as a result of her disobedience to God for eating the forbidden fruit. The two-fold consequence affected two significant roles in a woman's life: motherhood and marriage.

God's plan for marriage was tainted by Adam and Eve's sin and consequently, a tormenting battle between husband and wife exists. In the verse, the word "desire" means control. In essence, the wife will attempt to control her husband and he will attempt to dominate her; hence, a battle of the sexes. Unfortunately, there is nothing you can do to end this ongoing battle. Nevertheless, you can prevent it from overtaking your marriage by defining and fulfilling your roles.

One evening after a premarital counseling session on this subject, Marcus and I went our separate ways to complete our homework assignment. We were given a list of routine chores and were instructed to indicate whether we believed the husband or the wife should complete the chore. Our responses would indicate how we viewed each other's role in the marriage. In the end, our gender role assignments were similar to how we had both been raised: the husband takes care of everything outside the home while the wife takes care of everything inside the home.

Likewise, you should have a personal characterization of the wife's role and how you will execute it. Additionally, consider a personal characterization of a husband's role and how you imagine it. With an established idea of your role and areas you can be flexible or inflexible, you can easily discern applicable men and whether you complement them or not. Here are some common gender roles you may consider:

Trait/Chore	Husband	Wife	Neither
Cooking			
Cleaning			
Laundry			
Grocery shopping			
Lawn care			
Car repairs/maintenance			

Conversely, there are other gender roles that are not always considered but are just as important. These are the roles that may not appear until you are married. Here are some common, yet underlying, roles to consider:

Trait/Chore	Husband	Wife	Neither
Parenting			
Initiating sexual intimacy			
Working			
Breadwinner			
Bills/Banking			
Planning vacations, dates, etc.			

Although the idea of Marcus caring for the things outside the home while I cared for the things inside the home seemed ideal before marriage, it was not ideal once we were married. There was no flexibility. I neglected to offer flexibility because I did not consider that he or I might need help to fulfill our roles. There were countless occasions I requested his help to fulfill my defined roles whenever I was not feeling well, busy at work or simply overwhelmed. In turn, he also needed my help. Defining roles helps to delegate responsibilities only; it does not eliminate the need for flexibility.

Today, we understand we do not have to be as rigid and stiff, we can be flexible and understand some roles may be crossed and filled by the other; especially if it is all to the benefit of our family.

Values

Values are not often discussed in relationships. Instead, values are typically implied or assumed. Yet, it is better to discuss values openly rather than make an assumption about a person's standards. For example, you cannot afford to presume he is a family man because he talks to his mother often or he is a good provider because he has stable employment, you need to verify your beliefs. Moreover, an open discussion offers the chance to unite and agree on values you may want to relinquish, continue or initiate. You may begin the discussion with the following questions:

- ☐ What are your core values?
- ☐ Where do your values originate? Past experiences? Family? Religion?
- ☐ What values do you want to uphold in marriage?

- How will those values impact our desire to expand our family and raise children?

Do not limit the conversation to surface-level questions, dig deeper:

- How important are affirmations to you?
- Do you believe married couples should do everything together?
- Do you believe married couples can pursue individual interests?
- What is your stance on drinking?
- How important is it to have our individual friends?
- What is your stance on friends of the opposite sex?

Growing up with a father who worked tirelessly to provide for his family taught me one thing: I wanted my husband to be home making memories with our family more than I desired him to work tirelessly to provide. As a child, I had everything I wanted and more. Still, there were moments I wanted my father to witness but work obligations prohibited it. I wanted him to enjoy the fruits of his labor, the opportunities I was given as a result of his hard work.

This was a core value I hid in my heart until it was time to be revealed. During our engagement, Marcus and I talked extensively about this particular value. I wanted him to clearly understand the children we planned to have would not be raised by their mother alone. I wanted them to know and experience their parents equally.

Even though I shared this particular value with Marcus, I failed to investigate his. Instead, I presumed to know his values because we shared the same family structure, religious beliefs, traditions, etc. It was not until we were married I discovered the extent of his value regarding *meaningful* quality time. While I was satisfied being home together watching TV or reading a book while he watched a movie, he preferred to spend time together doing something adventurous such as going to dinner or playing board games.

"What's wrong with just spending time with me?" I asked.

"Nothing's wrong with that," he replied. "I just don't want to sit home all the time."

"Oh, so you need a distraction to have fun with me?" I concluded.

"That's not what I said," he answered. "Besides, you're always on your phone whenever we're home. You're not even paying attention to me."

"I do pay attention to you," I declared. "I'm just multitasking. Checking social media is how I wind down."

"Look, you like to spend time with me one way and I like to spend time with you another way. I just want to try it my way sometime," he explained. "That's all."

I cannot tell you how many times I got offended about this. As much as I got offended, Marcus had to reassure me about his intentions. How exhausting it must have been! Since I had not identified his values previously, I did not recognize this value whenever it appeared. Instead, I was busy thinking too deeply, trying to rationalize irrational thoughts, and conjuring unnecessary conflict. In the end, it was simply a matter of expressing similar values differently.

Even so, I failed to voice other values such as having a balanced life of work and play. It was easy for me to maintain a healthy balance because I worked forty hours a week, five days a week. My schedule was standard and easier to operate. After I worked my eight hours, I arrived home around the same time every day and was free to spend as much time together as available.

On the contrary, as a musician, Marcus' schedule was both routine and sporadic. Despite the spontaneity of his weekly schedule, he managed a comfortable balance. That is, until he booked larger-scale events such as weeklong conferences, live recordings, concerts, and conducting performances. During those instances, I was unhappy with his balancing act. Subsequently, each time an event of this magnitude rose, we argued faithfully.

"You always do this," he accused. "Every single time."

"Do what?" I asked.

"Every time I have something huge going on, you make it hard for me." He answered. "I'm already stressed about what I need to remember and what I need to do. You're making it worse."

"No, don't blame it on me," I snapped. "This is happening because you seem to forget that you have a wife at home when you're busy with work."

"I know I have a wife at home," he shot back. "That's why I'm working so hard."

"You're working so hard that you can't even call or text me? You're working too hard." I spat. "You remember the format of all those songs and the keys they're in but you can't remember to call me?"

"You're right, I should've called you," he admitted. "I'm sorry, I got caught up."

"You should be able to work and still maintain your priorities," I continued. "I work forty hours a week replying to emails, returning phone calls, going to meetings, working on projects and I still call or text you throughout the day. Why is it so hard for you to do the same? Because you have a lot going on right now?"

"I'm sorry," he repeated.

We rehashed this same argument again and again; at least twice a year. Looking back, I should have expressed my value of maintaining a balanced life of work and play. Actually, I should have taken it a step further and admitted how it made me feel if there was no balance or if it was not maintained. Regrettably, I did not have that discussion with my husband until I wrote this book. As a result, many of the most exciting career opportunities he has achieved since we have been married have been marred with images of terrible arguing and bitter remarks.

Open discussion about values eliminates the chance of having competing or opposing standards in the relationship. It identifies potential deal breakers before they affect the bond. It is better to learn at the start of the relationship that he values money over quality time or long-standing family traditions rather than creating new traditions with you. Additionally, honesty offers the possibility of fulfillment. I have no doubt that if I had been forthcoming and detailed about my values from the beginning that as my husband, Marcus would have met my needs.

« CONFESS YOUR FAULTS »

Verses to live by:

✓ *"Wherever your treasure is, there the desires of your heart will also be."* *Matthew 6:21 NLT*

✓ **"Guard your heart above all else, for it determines the course of your life."** *Proverbs 4:23 NLT*

✓ **"For as he thinks in his heart, so is he..."** Proverbs 23:7 NKJV

Yes/No

1. Do you have an established family plan?

2. Do you have a personal definition of what it means to be a wife?

3. Can you describe the type of man you want to marry?

4. Are you willing to adjust your values for the sake of unity and the bond of peace?

5. Can you identify your current values you want to continue in marriage?

Prayer: Holy Spirit, bless my marriage with the family You design especially for me. Help me to fulfill the role of a wife skillfully and with wisdom. Establish values built upon Your word within me and remove the contrary. Amen.

Confession: "My family structure will be set up according to what my relationship requires – not tradition."

Confession 3: Money

"After a failed attempt to manage our finances using control methods, I confess that a mutual understanding of budgeting, saving and spending, in addition to adequate personal financial stability, is essential for a Godly-successful marriage."

My mother majored in accounting in college. I grew up watching her balance her checkbook weekly on grid paper. It always appeared to be a time-consuming task. I secretly vowed to never balance my account using that method; I was sure there was another way.

When I got older, my mother taught my sister and I how to balance a checkbook with a check register instead of the grid paper. Then, she introduced the concept of saving, spending and giving. She bought three containers and labeled them accordingly. We were supposed to fill each container, as we desired with our weekly allowance.

The "giving" container was easy. We were taught as children about returning tithe and giving offering. The "spending" container would have been another simple decision if the "savings" container was not also present. It was always difficult to decide whether I wanted to make the most of my money now or later. Eventually, I developed a rhythm and put money in each container weekly. I learned it was always best to put money in my "savings" container no matter the amount.

I continued my saving, spending and giving money routine into adulthood. I ate good, shopped often and still had a savings to help whenever unexpected expenses arose. I was happy to not have to rely on my parents so heavily. Still, I was happy when Marcus moved to what later became our new hometown. His move meant I would have added stability.

When word spread that Marcus and I were engaged, there were many naysayers, both family and friends, who did not agree with his pursuit of a career in music. "That's not stable income. He needs a steady job," some declared. "There's no future in music. How will he take care of you?" others asked. However, his career never made me feel financially insecure. My outlook was quite the opposite.

In all the years I had been with Marcus, he had never been without a job. If he had an unexpected expense he always found a gig to make the extra money. Unlike me, I was never able to make extra money unless I got another job or worked overtime. Subsequently, I liked the fast money Marcus' career offered. When we got married, I did not have to worry about money because he could always make the money with an extra gig here or there.

With this sense of relief, I neglected my personal money routine and exchanged it for his. The problem was, Marcus did not have a rountine. Instead, he believed because he worked hard, he had every right to spend his money how he pleased. While I agreed he deserved to pamper himself, our savings took the hit. Month after month, we gave and spent without attempting to save.

I felt as if we were living dangerously without a savings. The lack of stability was unnerving for me but Marcus was always optimistic. He lived on the brigther side of the matter. I was fine not addressing the problem sternly until a large, unexpected expense emerged. Since we did not have the money in the bank, we had to do something we had been able to avoid until then: ask our parents for money.

As a result, I developed a budget without Marcus' input and monitored his purchasing activity closely. Supervising his spending was exhausting and he hated it. In hindsight, my behavior and independent decision-making undermined him as my cover. But, I did not grasp this fact until later. So, I tried to implement an allowance based on an amount I determined. That failed too.

The state of our finances did not improve until I expressed my concerns and anxieties to Marcus. To learn our finances were causing me to worry, which has other effects, he made it clear he wanted to allieviate me of the stress. Subsequently, we created a monthly budget that included bills, personal expenses and a savings goal. It was hard to adjust to the budget following a carefree lifestyle. However, it has kept us from finanical ruin.

Money Talk

During our engagement, the extent of our conversations about money was that we wanted to share accounts for accountability and transparency purposes. We also decided I would manage our finances, bills and banking because I was better organized. Internally, I had decided to follow my mother's philosophy about finances. Since my husband was going to be our chief provider, the last thing I wanted him to be concerned about was paying the bills. I put the bills in his name to denote his authority, however, I provided my contact information. I wanted him to work hassle-free and not be contacted regarding billing and banking concerns.

Money may be an uncomfortable topic to discuss but it is essential. Why? Money is a leading cause of divorce. Think about it, if you and your husband cannot decide how to earn, spend or save your income, working as a team will be challenging. Hence, you must discuss your individual finances to steer clear of debt and overspending. You may ask:

- When it comes to money, are you a saver or spender?
- What are your financial goals?
- What is your current financial status? Account balances? Debt? Retirement savings? Investments?
- Do you have a monthly budget including bills and personal expenses?
- How much money do you put aside for emergency funds, personal savings, etc.?
- Would you prefer to combine or separate our incomes?

- Who do you think should be responsible for paying the bills? Or, do you want to split the bill payments? If so, how?
- Do you think we should have a joint checking account, separate accounts or both?
- Should we lend money to family and friends? If so, how much?

Many believe discussing money is also intrusive. This may be due to their relationship with money or their understanding of money. Some people have a negative relationship with money as a result of mismanagement, fraud or socioeconomic status. As a result, money is viewed as a luxury rather than a necessity. With this theory in mind, talking about money to some would be equivalent to asking a person why their house or car is not bigger and better.

Others recognize money as an evil that generates a selfish pursuit of riches. People support this idea by denouncing their wealth or surrendering their worldly possessions. However, money itself is not the evil. On the contrary, *"...the love of money is a root of all kinds of evil, for which some have strayed from the faith in their greediness, and pierced themselves through with many sorrows." (I Timothy 6:10 NKJV)* The desire for wealth and riches, instead of being content with what God provides, creates the evil.

If we truly understood the purpose of money, we would absolutely ensure financial compatibility in addition to spiritual, mental and physical compatibility. *"For wisdom is a defense as money is a defense, But the excellence of knowledge is that wisdom gives life to those who have it." (Ecclesiastes 7:12 NKJV)* We need money. It is a crucial resource in the Earth because it offers security. Moreover*, "A feast is made for laughter, And wine makes merry; But money answers everything." (Ecclesiastes 10:19 NKJV)* Although money does not literally solve everything, it does help us to deal with various struggles.

« CONFESS YOUR FAULTS »

Verses to live by:

✓ "Not that I was ever in need, for I have learned how to be content with whatever I have. I know how to live on almost nothing or with everything. I have learned the secret of living in every situation, whether it is with a full stomach or empty, with plenty or little." *Philippians 4:11-12 NLT*

✓ "Once I was young, and now I am old. Yet I have never seen the godly abandoned or their children begging for bread." *Psalms 37:25 NLT*

✓ "If you start thinking to yourselves, "I did all this. And all by myself. I'm rich. It's all mine!"—well, think again. Remember that God, your God, gave you the strength to produce all this wealth so as to confirm the covenant that he promised to your ancestors—as it is today." *Deuteronomy 8:17-18 MSG*

Yes/No

1. Do you have measurable financial goals?

2. Are you financially stable?

3. Do you have a monthly budget to manage your finances?

4. Do you have a healthy perception of money?

5. Do you control your money or does it control you?

Prayer: Holy Spirit, help me to trust You with my money. Give me wisdom and discernment to effectively plan my financial future. Direct me in every way; show me where to spend, where to invest and how to save. Amen.

Confession: "I will not build my future upon an illusion of stability but I will be financially fit to know it is real."

Confession 2: Sex

"After learning and experiencing the work sexual intimacy requires, I confess that a healthy, vibrant and consistent sexual relationship with your husband is necessary for a Godly-successful marriage."

Yes! Let's talk about sex! Like me, maybe you have been taught sex is a subject discussed between husband and wife only. However, I believe waiting to discuss sex until you are married is too late. There are areas where personal decisions or preliminary discussions are warranted prior to marriage, before professional marriage counseling is needed to salvage the marriage.

I have had many group discussions with wives young and old, the consensus seems to be the same- a healthy, vibrant, and consistent sexual relationship takes work. Whether you are experienced or inexperienced, work is required. I know the entertainment culture illustrates that once we meet "the one" chemistry is automatic, like a magnetic attraction. However, chemistry requires work to maintain and overcome what time together may bring.

Honestly, the extent of the conversations Marcus and I had about sex before marriage was that we could not wait to have sex. I felt his simplest kisses in my toes, I felt a tingle in my spine whenever he whispered in my ear, and I melted under his stares. Despite these seemingly innocent actions and our good intentions, they always illuminated our sexual chemistry.

Of course, we knew about each other's beliefs and experiences but it was not until we were in a premarital counseling session that I realized sex would be more than pleasure, it would also be work. That was the first time I had heard about sex in a way that combated everything I had ever seen on TV or heard in music.

Contrary to popular belief, do not wait until premarital counseling or marriage to discuss sex. Why wait until marriage to discover what your husband thinks about sex and its role in marriage? Start the conversation as soon as the relationship warrants it, you may ask:

- Are you comfortable discussing sex?
- Are you comfortable discussing sexual likes and dislikes?
- What does a healthy sex life in marriage look like to you?
- How will you keep your thoughts pure until the wedding night?
- Are you comfortable with initiating intimacy?
- How will you initiate intimacy?
- How will you deal with times when you want sex and I do not?
- What will you do if your physical needs are not being met?
- How can we sustain the passion as our marriage progresses?
- Do you have any concerns about my previous relationships?

Myths

Growing up in church, sex was always a taboo topic. If you had any questions about it you were either told, "Just don't do it," or "Wait until you're married." As women, they taught us to "Keep our dresses long and our panties up." For the guys, my husband said he was mainly taught to protect himself. However, they did not teach us what to do with our panties when we got married. Similarly, my husband really was not told what to do after making sure he was protected. They preached a message of abstinence, but they never taught us how to control natural urges until marriage or the importance of sex in marriage. Needless to say, I am confessing here, I needed to have a serious, almost explicit, conversation about sex prior to our wedding night.

Conversation does not equal encouragement. Similarly, information and education does not invalidate your innocence or expose your guilt. Whatever the church does not address through Biblical scripture, people will learn from the world. Though it is not the church's responsibility to teach believers about sex, it should provide a platform for education. Unfortunately, since there is no platform, the world's perverse point of view is broadcasted through television, music and entertainment. In turn, the culture has become the sex educators and the standard regarding the matter. As a result, the world has birthed a generation of men and women who indulge in fornication, perversion, addictive behaviors, promiscuity and more.

In the absence of Biblical teaching and education about sex, some believers have settled for assumptions. Instead of admitting ignorance, they would rather believe an untruth. Although there are many legends about sex, here are five universal myths:

MYTH #1

Sex is for reproduction only.

Despite the suppression from the church, God created us as sexual beings. Thus, sex is a gift from God; it is a good gift. *"Do not be deceived, my beloved brethren. Every good gift and every perfect gift is from above, and comes down from the Father of lights, with whom there is no variation or shadow of turning."* *(James 1:16-17 NKJV)*

Sex is designed for enjoyment within the bond of marriage. In addition to reproduction, God created sex for several reasons:

1. **Physical intimacy:** *"Therefore a man shall leave his father and mother and be joined to his wife, and they shall become one flesh." (Genesis 2:24 NKJV)*

2. **Comfort:** *"And the servant told Isaac all the things that he had done. Then Isaac brought her into his mother Sarah's tent; and he took Rebekah and she became his wife, and he loved her. So Isaac was comforted after his mother's death." (Genesis 24:66-67 NKJV)*

3. **Reproduction:** *"Then God blessed them, and God said to them, 'Be fruitful and multiply; fill the earth and subdue it; have dominion over the fish of the sea, over the birds of the air, and over every living thing that moves on the earth.'" (Genesis 1:28 NKJV)*

4. **Pleasure:** *"Behold, you are fair, my love! Behold, you are fair! You have dove's eyes behind your veil. Your hair is like a flock of goats, going down from Mount Gilead. Your teeth are like a flock of shorn sheep which have come up from the washing, every one of which bears twins, and none is barren among them. Your lips are like a strand of scarlet, and your mouth is lovely. Your temples behind your veil are like a piece of pomegranate. Your neck is like the tower of David, built for an armory, on which hang a thousand bucklers, all shields of mighty men. Your two breasts are like two fawns, twins of a gazelle, which feed among the lilies. Until the day breaks and the shadows flee*

away, I will go my way to the mountain of myrrh and to the hill of frankincense. You are all fair, my love, and there is no spot in you. Come with me from Lebanon, my spouse, with me from Lebanon. Look from the top of Amana, from the top of Senir and Hermon, from the lions' dens, from the mountains of the leopards. You have ravished my heart, my sister, my spouse; you have ravished my heart with one look of your eyes, with one link of your necklace. How fair is your love, my sister, my spouse! How much better than wine is your love, and the scent of your perfumes than all spices! Your lips, O my spouse, drip as the honeycomb; honey and milk are under your tongue; and the fragrance of your garments is like the fragrance of Lebanon. A garden enclosed is my sister, my spouse, a spring shut up, a fountain sealed. Your plants are an orchard of pomegranates with pleasant fruits, fragrant henna with spikenard, Spikenard and saffron, Calamus and cinnamon, with all trees of frankincense, Myrrh and aloes, with all the chief spices— A fountain of gardens, a well of living waters, and streams from Lebanon. Awake, O north wind, and come, O south! Blow upon my garden, that its spices may flow out. Let my beloved come to his garden and eat its pleasant fruits." (Song of Solomon 4:1-16 NKJV)

5. **Escape temptation:** *"Do not deprive one another except with consent for a time, that you may give yourselves to fasting and prayer; and come together again so that Satan does not tempt you because of your lack of self-control."* *(I Corinthians 7:5 NKJV)*

MYTH #2
Sex is too sacred to discuss outside the covenant of marriage.

If we limit the discussion of sex to marriage only, we forfeit the opportunity to accurately inform and prepare singles for the marital responsibility. For many, including me, the struggle to remain abstinent in an over sexualized world was strenuous. By acknowledging the struggle and equipping singles with tools to avoid fornication, dismantles the silence, secrecy and shame surrounding sex. In turn, husbands and wives can broach the subject without fear.

This myth also extends the idea that questions or concerns about sex cannot be communicated to external resources. This stigma must be demolished so if necessary, husbands and wives can be comfortable speaking with a doctor, counselor or therapist regarding issues that may affect their sexual health. For this cause, marriages suffer from an unfulfilling sex life due to shame.

MYTH #3

A past of fornication and/or promiscuity makes you undesirable to other men.

This popular lie created and spread by the enemy to condemn and devalue. It breeds deceitful thinking such as, "Once a whore, always a whore." Or, "Once a liar, always a liar." Now, this is true for unbelievers as there is no exoneration for their sin. Yet, this is not true for believers. *"For He made Him who knew no sin to be sin for us, that we might become the righteousness of God in Him." (II Corinthians 5:21 NKJV)* In fact, God is so unbothered about the potential of your past infecting your future that He *"...demonstrates His own love toward us, in that while we were still sinners, [He] died for us." (Romans 5:8 NKJV)*

If you have a personal relationship with Jesus Christ and are led by the Holy Spirit, He does not confine you to your past. Neither does He define you by your past. *"There is therefore now no condemnation to those who are in Christ Jesus, who do not walk according to the flesh, but according to the Spirit." (Romans 8:1 NKJV)* Believers are not bound to their sinful past because Christ's crucifixion pardoned us. Consequently, we are given a new identity *by* Him and *in* Him. *"Therefore, if anyone is in Christ, he is a new creation; old things have passed away; behold, all things have become new." (II Corinthians 5:17 NKJV)* Whether the world accepts or respects your new identity, they can do nothing to remove or destroy it. *"Therefore if the Son makes you free, you shall be free indeed." (John 8:36 NKJV)*

MYTH #4

"I need to know what I'm doing on my wedding night."

"Did you buy new underwear yet?" My mother asked.

"What do you mean?" I asked, shocked by the conversation.

"You're getting married in a few days," she explained. "You're not going to that man's house with the same underwear you've been wearing since high school."

"Okay," I hesitated. "I was given lingerie as gifts at the bridal shower. Some of the pieces came with underwear."

"That's not enough," she concluded. "What about pajamas?"

"Well, when I'm not wearing lingerie I can put on a t-shirt and shorts, right?"

"The same cheerleading t-shirts and shorts you've been wearing since high school? Girl, please," my mother sucked her teeth, walking toward the lingerie section of the store.

That conversation with my mother shook me. After 22 years of purity and suppression, how was I supposed to magically be sexy? Tempting? Alluring? How was I supposed to suddenly shift my thinking from "sex is wrong" to "sex is right" after the ceremony? I felt as if I had been requested for a performance I agreed to do, even wanted to do, but never had the opportunity to prepare. I knew Marcus would be expecting to experience a side of me I had never met on our wedding night. A side of me I was not sure I possessed or could summon.

After many years of waiting, I wanted to meet my husband's expectations. I even began contemplating whether we should have sex before the ceremony to guarantee our wedding night would be everything we imagined. Thankfully, the Holy Spirit reminded me the experience would be more satisfying because Marcus loved me and was committing himself to me before Him and everyone we loved. Although premarital sex seems like the remedy for an awkward wedding night, sex before marriage creates memories and connections with someone who may not be your husband. *"Let integrity and uprightness preserve me, For I wait for You." (Psalms 25:21 NKJV)*

Additionally, if you are a virgin, it only intensifies the symbolism of the wedding night. The physical union signifies the cutting of two bodies to become one flesh. Literally, for a virgin, the cutting is visible through the shedding of your blood. Like wedding rings, the bloodstain is another physical sign of covenant. Virginity is so highly regarded in some cultures that the sheets from the bridal bed are proudly displayed after consummation.

MYTH #5

Sex is miraculously fulfilling and easy when you get married.

Ha! In my opinion, this is one of the biggest lies about sex. Moreover, it has deceived many married couples. I know because I was one of the many who believed the lie. You would think all the physical and sexual chemistry between you and your husband would translate both naturally and easily into the bedroom, right? Wrong. If you believe this myth you deprive yourself from fully indulging into an adventure-filled, exploratory sexual journey with your husband. Further, you give space to the enemy to sow seeds of separation, discontentment and more if sexual satisfaction is not inherent. Marriage creates a covering for honorable sexual intimacy only; it does not automatically guarantee sexual satisfaction.

Even if you marry the man created especially for you, sex is a learned activity. It requires more than natural desires and the participation of a willing man and woman. It does not matter how many times you have had sex in the past or how many partners you have had, it is still a learned activity. For example, despite the athleticism of your favorite athlete, they too must practice to perfect their natural abilities. Regardless of the years they have played their sport, learning, modifying and practicing are nonstop requirements.

Similarly, you and your husband will have to commit to constant learning and practicing to achieve mutually fulfilling sexual intimacy. However, the reality is that the ease or difficulty of the learning process varies per couple. Still, there will never be a time in which you will stop learning due to changing components and unforeseen circumstances such as body language, the frequency required, likes, dislikes, health, career, children, etc. For this reason, patience and understanding is needed. Therefore, *"....let patience have its perfect work, that you may be perfect and complete, lacking nothing." (James 1:4 NKJV)*

Duty Bound

In addition to the purposes of sex, it is also an obligation within marriage. *"Let the husband render to his wife the affection due her, and likewise also the wife to her husband. The wife does not have authority over her own body, but the husband does. And likewise the husband does not have authority over his own body, but the wife does." (I Corinthians 7:3-4 NKJV)* Husbands and wives are obligated to provide the sexual enjoyment the other is entitled to receive under the covenant of marriage.

Sex is both expected and healthy for the life of a marriage. Biblical principles advise a regular routine of sexual pleasure to avoid the temptation to find satisfaction outside of marriage. *"No temptation has overtaken you except such as is common to man; but God is faithful, who will not allow you to be tempted beyond what you are able, but with the temptation will also make the way of escape, that you may be able to bear it." (I Corinthians 10:13 NKJV)* Sex- not control, tracking devices, or distrustful behavior such as inspecting phones, pants pockets, mileage, etc.- is the way of escape provided.

While the Bible does not prescribe a number or level of frequency, it should be consistent. It should also be equal, mutual and as frequently as each requires. The Bible teaches us to govern ourselves, even in sexual pleasure, by the principle of self-sacrifice. *"Let nothing be done through selfish ambition or conceit, but in lowliness of mind let each esteem others better than himself. Let each of you look out not only for his own interests, but also for the interests of others." (Philippians 2:3-4 NKJV)* Husbands and wives should not engage in sexual intimacy that is dangerous, demeaning or offensive to one another. Instead, sex should be mutually safe, pleasurable and fulfilling.

Sexual intimacy requires permission and demands participation from both the husband and the wife. Specifically, regarding the wife, God commands the husband to:

1. Find satisfaction: *"As a loving deer and a graceful doe, Let her breasts satisfy you at all times; And always be enraptured with her love."* (Proverbs 5:19 NKJV)

2. Find joy: *"Live joyfully with the wife whom you love all the days of your vain life which He has given you under the sun, all your days of vanity; for that is your portion in life, and in the labor which you perform under the sun."* (Ecclesiastes 9:9 NKJV)

3. Meet her needs: *"Husbands, likewise, dwell with them with understanding, giving honor to the wife, as to the weaker vessel, and as being heirs together of the grace of life, that your prayers may not be hindered."* (I Peter 3:7 NKJV)

Equally, regarding the husband, God commands the wife to:

1. Prepare and plan to secure his heart: *"The voice of my beloved! Behold, he comes leaping upon the mountains, skipping upon the hills. My beloved is like a gazelle or a young stag. Behold, he stands behind our wall; he is looking through the windows, gazing through the lattice. My beloved spoke, and said to me: "Rise up, my love, my fair one, and come away. For lo, the winter is past, the rain*

is over and gone. The flowers appear on the earth; the time of singing has come, and the voice of the turtledove is heard in our land. The fig tree puts forth her green figs, and the vines with the tender grapes give a good smell. Rise up, my love, my fair one, and come away! "O my dove, in the clefts of the rock, in the secret places of the cliff, let me see your face, let me hear your voice; for your voice is sweet, and your face is lovely." (Song of Solomon 2:8-14 NKJV)

2. **Display sexual interest:** *"I sleep, but my heart is awake; it is the voice of my beloved! He knocks, saying, 'Open for me, my sister, my love, my dove, my perfect one; for my head is covered with dew, my locks with the drops of the night.'" (Song of Solomon 5:2 NKJV)*

3. **Be attentive to his unique masculine needs:** *"Then Isaac brought her into his mother Sarah's tent; and he took Rebekah and she became his wife, and he loved her. So Isaac was comforted after his mother's death." (Genesis 24:67 NKJV)*

I have met wives who have limited their sexual pleasure with their husbands due to erroneous counsel from church people. One wife admitted, "I was taught it is wrong to have sex in any other position except with my husband on top." Another disclosed,

"I was taught sex does not require lingerie, music, massage oils, etc." My advice? Endeavor to meet your husband's sexual needs, not the needs or counsel of people. Many marriages have failed because they carried the expectations and counsel of others into their bedroom.

Sex is the most powerful form of physical intimacy to create one flesh. It is the sincerest form of spiritual harmony between a man and a woman as well. An unhealthy sexual relationship in a marriage is like an open wound. The longer the wound is left untreated, infection appears and festers, infecting surrounding areas. By the time the wound is finally treated, basic aid is no longer suffient; professional help is required.

"My people are destroyed for lack of knowledge..." (Hosea 4:6 NKJV) It is the enemy's desire that you remain oblivious to the responsibility and role of sex in marriage. Yet, oblivion does not exempt you from the danger that will surface if you do not grasp the importance of sex in marriage. Furthermore, remaining ill informed increases the enemy's chances of dissolving Godly marriages and therefore limiting the reproduction of new life in the likeness of God. For this reason, you must have preliminary discussions in relationships and endeavor to be informed and educated about sex prior to marriage ***"...lest Satan should take advantage of [you]; for we are not ignorant of his devices." (II Corinthians 2:11 NKJV)***

« CONFESS YOUR FAULTS »

Verses to live by:

✓ *"Marriage is honorable among all, and the bed undefiled; but fornicators and adulterers God will judge."* Hebrews 13:4 NKJV

✓ *"Run from anything that stimulates youthful lusts. Instead, pursue righteous living, faithfulness, love, and peace. Enjoy the companionship of those who call on the LORD with pure hearts."* II Timothy 2:22 NLT

✓ *"Let your fountain be blessed, And rejoice with the wife of your youth."* Proverbs 5:18 NKJV

Yes/No

1. Can you define what a healthy sex life in marriage looks like to you?

2. Do you understand mutual sexual satisfaction is the goal?

3. Do you understand "sex is right" within the covenant of marriage?

4. Do you understand sex is not a weapon but a gift?

5. Do you understand patience and understanding are essential for sexual intimacy?

Prayer: Holy Spirit, despite my past, help me to move from shame to freedom. You gave me this natural desire so I trust that You can and will provide the tools to employ self-control as necessary. May I satisfy my husband always and may he always be intoxicated with my love. Amen.

Confession: "Sex in my marriage will be governed by my husband and I, not the church and built upon Biblical truths."

Confession 1: God

"After relying on a form of godliness, I confess that the husband and wife must have individual, consistent relationships with God for a Godly-successful marriage."

I know what you must be thinking, "We discussed this already!" Well, we examined church and religion in an earlier confession. But, we only touched the surface. We need to dig deeper.

You may believe this is the most obvious, self-explanatory confession in the entire book. In fact, you may be wondering why it is even a chapter. If these are your thoughts, that is the very reason this confession was included. This may be one of the most common assumptions in marriage, if not the biggest, when you are with someone who attends church or claims to be "spiritual." Too often we assume because our husband or fiancé believes in God, it means they also have a relationship with Him. Unfortunately, this assumption is simply not true.

Since Marcus and I grew up in the same church, I had concluded that God was not a dating requirement we had to address once we were engaged. I knew Marcus believed in God and he knew I felt the same. Moreover, we did not simply believe God existed, we believed in His word. To me, it was a settled matter, no need for discussion. We talked about God, shared the same beliefs, and even had our own version of couple's Bible study from time to time. That was enough, right?

Shortly after we married and the glitz and glamour of newlywed bliss had dissolved, it was clear that *knowing* God was not sufficient. I quickly realized that an individual, ongoing relationship with God was needed to help me fulfill my role as a wife. There were numerous instances in which I disrespected Marcus because he fell short of my expectations. Despite my deep love for him, I could not keep my submission in check whenever he disappointed. It remained in limbo. Do you know why? It takes the power of God, through the Holy Spirit, to obey and submit to your husband.

What am I saying? Do not assume your husband has a personal relationship with God because he "knows" Him. How many people do you know that you do not have a personal relationship with? Regardless of his level of church attendance or even his title, be sure he has a relationship. Confirm it. Attend church with him and observe how he participates in the worship service.

- Is he attentive or distracted?
- Does he appear interested or bored?
- Does he bring his Bible?
- Does he take notes?
- Does the Word convict him?
- Does he strive to live accordingly in areas he is weak?
- Does he read his Bible outside of church?
- Does he have personal prayer and/or devotional time?

I remember a friend who observed her crush in church after the congregation erupted in worship. The first time she observed him rubbing his eyes, he seemed to be distracted. The next time she observed him, his hands were raised in adoration. There was another friend who went to church with her boyfriend and observed him texting throughout the worship experience, noticeably uninterested in what was happening around him. Observations such as these may confirm whether a personal relationship exists and possibly the depth of the relationship.

Personal Conviction

A personal relationship with Jesus Christ founded upon a personal experience is vital. You are more likely to believe and declare what you have encountered firsthand. *"Oh, taste and see that the LORD is good; Blessed is the man who trusts in Him!" (Psalms 34:8 NKJV)* I know the Lord is a protector because there were accidents I should have experienced due to my negligence. I know the Lord is a provider because when I did not have a job, my bills were paid and I never missed a meal. As a result of my immeasurable personal encounters with the Lord, my personal conviction is non-wavering.

God designed your husband to cover you as He covers man. Further, He designed your husband to lead and guide you as He leads and guides the body of Christ. The husband is able to effectively fulfill his role with Christ as his guide. *"But I want you to know that the head of every man is Christ, the head of woman is man, and the head of Christ is God." (I Corinthians 11:3 NKJV)* The mandate given to wives from husbands is, *"Imitate me, just as I also imitate Christ." (I Corinthians 11:1 NKJV)* Yet, if your husband does not have a personal relationship with Jesus Christ, whom will you imitate? What spirit or idol will you be imitating? Therefore, how can your husband truly be your head without knowing his head?

"Husbands, love your wives, just as Christ also loved the church and gave Himself for her, that He might sanctify and cleanse her with the washing of water by the word, that He might present her to Himself a glorious church, not having spot or wrinkle or any such thing, but that she should be holy and without blemish. So husbands ought to love their own wives as their own bodies; he who loves his wife loves himself. For no one ever hated his own flesh, but nourishes and cherishes it, just as the LORD *does the church." (Ephesians 5:25-29 NKJV)* The only way your husband can love you like Christ loves the church is to have a personal relationship with Christ. This type of love cannot be achieved in the flesh alone.

I know of wives who married a self-proclaimed believer who later converted to another religion. Naturally, it caused hardship in the marriage. How could she continue to submit to him if he submitted to another being? How could she continue to trust and follow his leadership if he received it from an idol? ***"For the time will come when they will not endure sound doctrine, but according to their own desires, because they have itching ears, they will heap up for themselves teachers; and they will turn their ears away from the truth, and be turned aside to fables." (II Timothy 4:3-4 NKJV)*** For this reason, personal conviction is supreme. It will prevent your husband from being led astray and in turn, lead you astray.

If you are currently married and your husband lacks a relationship with Christ or has left the faith, there is hope. ***"And a woman who has a husband who does not believe, if he is willing to live with her, let her not divorce him. For the unbelieving husband is sanctified by the wife, and the unbelieving wife is sanctified by the husband; otherwise your children would be unclean, but now they are holy." (I Corinthians 7:13-14 NKJV)*** Moreover, I am certain living a life of righteousness, honor and respect before an unbelieving husband will change his heart. ***"The Lᴏʀᴅ is not slack concerning His promise, as some count slackness, but is longsuffering toward us, not willing that any should perish but that all should come to repentance." (II Peter 3:9 NKJV)***

Marriage does not eliminate the need for individual relationships with Christ. This is essential to effectively satisfy your roles as husband and wife. In addition, the couple must cultivate a collective bond with Christ in which they uphold together through prayer and devotion. Placing Christ at the center anchors your marriage on a solid foundation. So, when the storms of life erupt, the marriage remains fixed on its foundation.

« CONFESS YOUR FAULTS »

Verses to live by:

✓ *"Therefore, brethren, be even more diligent to make your call and election sure, for if you do these things you will never stumble; for so an entrance will be supplied to you abundantly into the everlasting kingdom of our Lord and Savior Jesus Christ." II Peter 1:10 NKJV*

✓ *"For God so loved the world that He gave His only begotten Son, that whoever believes in Him should not perish but have everlasting life." John 3:16 NKJV*

✓ *"For by grace you have been saved through faith, and that not of yourselves; it is the gift of God, not of works, lest anyone should boast." Ephesians 2:8-9 NKJV*

Yes/No

1. Do you have a personal relationship with Jesus Christ?

2. Is your personal conviction regarding your salvation indisputable?

3. Do you understand church attendance or participation does not indicate relationship?

4. Do you understand God has designated you to sanctify the house if your husband is not a believer?

5. Do you understand you must maintain a steady relationship with Christ to succeed as a Godly wife?

Prayer: Holy Spirit, increase my capacity for You. Help me to discern Your spirit in others. Unite my spirit with that of my husband. Bind us together both physically and spiritually. Amen.

Confession: "Knowing the culture of church and participating in it is not a substitute for a personal relationship with Jesus Christ. I will seek to know Him for myself."

Ready. Set. Go!

I was never one of those women who had their wedding planned as a child. I was not obsessed with the idea of being married or the details of the ceremony. Nevertheless, I always assumed I would one day be a wife. Yet, instead of spending my singleness counting the costs regarding marriage, I expected to assume the role when it was time. I never imagined the transition would be challenging. I never took time to learn about the role, prepare for the role or ask the Holy Spirit to help me fulfill the role until I was a wife. I was so naïve. I hope you will learn from my scars and endeavor to develop regularities and resolve irregularities regarding these popular marital issues *before* you make the commitment.

I have spoken with many wives who said, "If I knew then what I know now," before stating their confession. Some admit they may have married someone else, waited to marry at a later age, finished school before marriage, had fewer or no children with their husband, and researched their husband's family more intensely. *"For which of you, intending to build a tower, does not sit down first and count the cost, whether he has enough to finish it– lest, after he has laid the foundation, and is not able to finish, all who see it begin to mock him, saying, 'This man began to build and was not able to finish'? Or what king, going to make war against another king, does not sit down first and consider whether he is able with ten thousand to meet him who comes against him with twenty thousand? Or else, while the other is still a great way off, he sends a delegation and asks conditions of peace." (Luke 14:28-32 NKJV)*

Similar to a person who does not anticipate the costs of construction before breaking ground or a king who does not seriously consider the odds before going to war and are mocked for beginning tasks they cannot finish, you too must understand and prepare for what marriage entails *before* you make the commitment. Once you are married, it may be difficult to remedy matters that could have been evaded altogether. Then, if these matters arise in marriage and a reasonable, mutually-beneficial solution cannot be formed to sustain the marriage, separation or divorce is deemed as the solution.

Ready.

Regrettably, culture insinuates that marriage should be achieved by a certain time in a woman's life. If not, the woman is deemed a "lonely spinster" or "man-hater." Subsequently, many women have married too soon or married the wrong man to avoid being alone and gain companionship. But, think about it. How successful will your marriage be if you are ill prepared for the journey or you are joining your life with an incompatible man to deny loneliness?

We are living in a time in which reality shows portray marriage as an easy, clinically proven, three-step process. It broadcasts the perception that marriage is an underrated feat. Yet, expert filming and editing only present a highlight reel of marriage; the outtakes are rarely broadcasted. Therefore, we tend to fall in love with the *idea* of marriage instead of the *reality* of marriage.

Since marriage is such a hot topic in our culture, it has become one of the most premier statuses to attain. TV is filled with unmarried, licensed professionals creating shows like ninety-day engagements, marrying strangers at first sight, or selecting a spouse from a group of strangers. These shows accelerate and abbreviate the dating and marriage processes for entertainment purposes. Although the acceleration secures ratings, the abbreviation often leaves participants with broken hearts, broken promises, broken spirits and broken marriages. In addition to verbal consent and "feeling ready," marriage involves physical, mental and spiritual preparation.

No matter what family, friends, society, or even the church advises, no one can corroborate your readiness for marriage except you, with the help of the Holy Spirit. Do not allow any person or institution to pressure or rush you into marriage. Further, no one should select your husband except you, with the help of the Holy Spirit. If you enter into the covenant of marriage without the help of the Holy Spirit, you are prone to be weakened by the work marriage requires. Consequently, your resolve to sustain the marriage is likely to wither and eventually, so will the marriage.

Set.

I pray *Confessions of a Virgin Bride* has provided you with a realistic view of Godly-successful marriage. The confessions of Communication, Church, In-Laws, Career, Family, Money, Sex and God are the major components of marriage most couples have to confront during their tenure. Even so, *"Catch us the foxes, The little foxes that spoil the vines, For our vines have tender grapes." (Song of Solomon 2:15 NKJV)* The sub-components within each major component possess the potential to be just as detrimental.

Marriage is honorable before God and the benefits are superb but it involves work. *"Unless the Lord builds the house, They labor in vain who build it; Unless the Lord guards the city, The watchman stays awake in vain." (Psalms 127:1 NKJV)* Unless Christ is at the center of the marriage, the husband and wife's labor to sustain the covenant is ineffective. Marriage requires the help of the Holy Spirit and Biblical wisdom for fruitfulness and longevity; this cannot be achieved through the flesh.

Like any process, change may generate discomfort. For example, the processes of pregnancy, losing weight or moving to a new city may all cause discomfort. Similarly, you can expect marriage to generate discomfort also known as "growing pains." *"If you faint in the day of adversity, Your strength is small." (Proverbs 24:10 NKJV)* Do not lose hope as a result of the pains; it is confirmation that change is taking place. Whether the pains change your marriage positively or negatively is up to you to decide.

Although marriage requires individual preparation, it is ultimately an interpersonal ministry. Husbands and wives attend to the needs of one another as a Pastor does for a church. They pledge to connect their lives and encourage, correct and help each other until death separates them. The purpose of marriage is so imperative you must strive to fulfill your role diligently. If not, you can push the very thing God created to love and cover you on the Earth, away. *"Better to dwell in a corner of a housetop, Than in a house shared with a contentious woman." (Proverbs 21:9 NKJV)* Or, you can cause your husband to lose joy and strength. *"An excellent wife is the crown of her husband, But she who causes shame is like rottenness in his bones." (Proverbs 12:4 NKJV)*

Go!

Growing up, I learned benediction was the most important part of the church service. "Don't ever leave before the benediction," my mother always warned. I never understood why as a child but I was always afraid to disobey her warning. Like church, this is the point of the book where we dismiss, go out into the world and apply what we have just learned. However, before our dismissal, let me take a moment to offer final words of hope and declare a blessing.

Marriage is an opportunity to show you who you are and transform you. Marriage has shown me I can be selfish, spoiled, naïve, inflexible and controlling. It has also shown me the depth of my love, the bounty of my forgiveness, the extent of my strength, and the degree of my patience. Finally, it has deepened my relationship with Christ, my reliance on the Holy Spirit, and my prayer life.

Obviously, I did not write this book because I am an expert concerning marriage. As you have read, I have made countless mistakes along the way. In fact, years later, there are some areas in which I am sharper than others. There have been times we have had arguments that shook the foundation of our marriage. In those times, I wonder how we ever made it this far. The enemy speaks louder in those moments, attempting to plant seeds of doubt, discord and even quitting. When I do not understand Marcus, I find solace in that *"He has made [his heart], so he understands everything [he does]." (Psalms 33:15 NLT)* Therefore, I remain confident about the future of my marriage because I am in relationship with the One who knows Marcus best.

"I'm not saying that I have this all together, that I have it made. But I am well on my way, reaching out for Christ, who has so wondrously reached out for me. Friends, don't get me wrong:

By no means do I count myself an expert in all of this, but I've got my eye on the goal, where God is beckoning us onward— to Jesus. I'm off and running, and I'm not turning back. So let's keep focused on that goal, those of us who want everything God has for us. If any of you have something else in mind, something less than total commitment, God will clear your blurred vision— you'll see it yet! Now that we're on the right track, let's stay on it."
(Philippians 3:12-16 MSG)

After reading *Confessions of a Virgin Bride*, I believe you too are well on your way. I pray the completion of these eight confessions will mark a new beginning for your marriage and your perception of marriage. I pray you will never be the same after the self-examination you have experienced while reading. I pray the scriptures you have read will be imprinted on your heart, fueling a regenerative source of hope when you need it most. *"For whatever things were written before were written for our learning, that we through the patience and comfort of the Scriptures might have hope." (Romans 15:4 NKJV)* I pray your husband will desire to change as a result of the change he witnesses in you. *"Now may the God of patience and comfort grant you to be like-minded toward one another, according to Christ Jesus, that you may with one mind and one mouth glorify the God and Father of our Lord Jesus Christ." (Romans 15:5-6 NKJV)* I pray your passion for one another will be rekindled and never extinguished.

143

"And the LORD said, '[Women!] Indeed, Satan has asked for you [and your marriages], that he may sift you as wheat. But I have prayed for you, that your faith should not fail; and when you have returned to Me, strengthen [another woman and/or wife]." *(Luke 22:31-32 NKJV)* Here's to raising up a generation of wise and informed women suitable for Godly-successful marriages! Amen.

Acknowledgments

Writing *Confessions of a Virgin Bride* was so hard! It challenged me mentally and emotionally because it dropped me into one of the most difficult seasons of my own marriage. There were countless days I did not feel worthy to advise others. I even questioned God about my right to counsel others given my apparent shortcomings. Yet, He reminded me what I have asked others who also doubted His will: "How would you know God was a healer if you have never been sick?" or "How would you know He was a deliverer if you have never been in trouble?" So, I had to ask myself, "How would you know God had the power to heal and restore marriages if your marriage had never been in trouble?" Kolanda, "How would you know the depth and totality of His power if you had never experienced it personally?" And, "How will you exude genuine compassion and provide trusted counsel without a personal testimony?"

Now I can declare, ***"It is good for me that I have been afflicted, That I may learn Your statutes." (Psalm 119:71 NKJV)*** Wow! I never thought I would ever say those words. Yet, if I am honest with myself, my affliction inspired this book. I struggled writing each confesssion. It was not that I was too embarassed to share my experiences, I have been freed from the shame of my past. Instead, it was because I re-encountered each confession prior to writing about it. Although it was very difficult to readdress and rework issues I wanted to help others combat, it was worth the sacrifice for your sake. It gave me the opportunity to personally exercise what the Lord had given me to share with you. Besides, it confirms my suffering was not in vain. It is a testimony of God's purposeful nature and His plans for my life. Therefore, first and foremost, my Lord and Savior, I am forever grateful. Great is thy faithfulness!

To my village readers, as always, your feedback and input is invaluable. Daddy, Mommy and Tee, thank you for your roles in the story of my life. Thank you for pushing me to continue when I desperately wanted to give up. Thank you for holding me accountable to God and the women who would need this resource. Mommy, you always told me marriage would teach me how to pray, I get it now!

To my son, you are my "why." Learning Daddy and I were expecting you woke me up from my dull, empty and fruitless existence. As a result, I am constantly dreaming and working to be someone you will be proud of. I pray what God accomplishes through me will be a lasting imprint in your heart of His goodness. Additionally, I pray that it is a constant reminder of what you too can accomplish if you allow God to *"...work in you both to will and to do for His good pleasure." (Philippians 2:13 NKJV)*

Finally, to my husband, my best friend and Superman, thank you for allowing me to be vulnerable and share our story with the world. As I wrote each confession, it was an interesting and emotional journey down memory lane. We have endured many things individually and collectively and yet, we were able to withstand. I recognize how much we have grown and how much our love has matured. Years ago we were two teenagers embarking on unknown territory to become young adults in love, wanting to share their lives together with no real clue about the work marriage required. And despite the learning curve, look at us now. Look at what we have achieved, what we have built, and what we have created. I look forward to a lifetime with you, I love you.

Kolanda